Four Steps to Mature Manhood

A new perspective on Paul's

Letter to the Ephesians

Loren VanGalder

Spiritual Father Publications

ISBN-10: 0-9976935-9-2

ISBN-13: 978-0-9976935-9-1

TABLE OF CONTENTS

DEDICATION

This book is dedicated to the pastors, churches, and fellow believers in Costa Rica. This book was born out of messages I was invited to give in a church in Bajo Rodriguez, Alajuela, Costa Rica, in January of 2014. In May of that year, we moved to Costa Rica. It has been a great privilege to be part of the Body of Christ in this beautiful country. ¡Pura Vida!

INTRODUCTION

I have always enjoyed the book of Ephesians:

- I was a new staff worker with InterVarsity Christian Fellowship in the late '70's when I heard IV's cross-cultural specialist, Thom Hoppler, give a unique perspective on the book in a series called "The Ephesus Zoo."
- Several years later, John Stott came out with his great book *God's New Society.*
- Using that book as a test, I designed a small group study course of Ephesians for use on New York City college campuses.

I never intended to write a book on Ephesians. I could not come close to Stott's classic, but when I had the opportunity to share a series of messages at a church in Costa Rica, I was led to Ephesians, and was struck by a progression in the second half of the book I had never noticed before. Given my current ministry of mentoring younger men, I was particularly struck by the goal stated in Ephesians 4:13: attaining mature manhood (that is what the Greek literally says, but of course more recent, politically correct translations, change "manhood" to make it more inclusive). The Amplified Bible says: *That [we might arrive] at really mature manhood (the completeness of personality which is nothing less than the standard height of Christ's own perfection).* Clearly, Paul does not have only men in mind. He is speaking in general about reaching Christian maturity. Yet the fact remains that, political correctness aside, Paul wrote about reaching mature manhood. That goal is a lofty one, yet the Bible assures us that God has provided the means to reach it. Sadly, the maturity Paul describes here is attained by very few. That is why I have been so impressed by the four steps clearly described in Ephesians 4-6, even though I shy away from books that promise "Three Keys to a Better Marriage," or some similar simplistic, formulaic approach to the complexities of life. I believe that making the teaching of Ephesians part of your life will be a giant step toward that mature manhood. And yes, this is written for men, but ladies, you will also benefit from it.

THE HISTORY OF THE CHURCH IN EPHESUS

We will start with a trip back to the first century, to one of the most impressive churches of that age. A Spirit-filled church that impacted the entire area, I believe it serves as a great model for us in the 21st century. Of course, we are more sophisticated, with our advanced technology. We feel we have it more together than people did thousands of years ago. History is not popular today; we are too busy thinking about the future. What could we possibly learn from them? A lot. We have failed to learn from the past, and keep repeating the same mistakes. We have lost something very important – which the Ephesian church also lost.

1 THE GOSPEL COMES TO EPHESUS

ACTS 18:24-28

Ephesus was an important, prosperous, commercial center of the Roman Empire, in what was then called Asia (today's Turkey). There was a significant Jewish population, but it was a very pagan city. The temple to Diana was one of the Seven Wonders of the Ancient World.

Paul had briefly stopped in the city and met some of the Jews, but then left, saying he would return if it was God's will. The church's history begins in Acts chapter 18, verses 24-28:

Meanwhile a Jew named Apollos, a native of Alexandria, came to Ephesus. He was a learned man, with a thorough knowledge of the Scriptures. He had been instructed in the way of the Lord, and he spoke with great fervor and taught about Jesus accurately, though he knew only the baptism of John. He began to speak boldly in the synagogue. When Priscilla and Aquila heard him, they invited him to their home and explained to him the way of God more adequately.

When Apollos wanted to go to Achaia, the brothers and sisters encouraged him and wrote to the disciples there to welcome him. When he arrived, he was a great help to those who by grace had believed. For he vigorously refuted his Jewish

9

opponents in public debate, proving from the Scriptures that Jesus was the Messiah.

The man God used to plant this church

God usually uses an anointed man to start a church. In this case it was Apollos. He was from Alexandria, Egypt, one of the most important cities in the Roman Empire. Here we learn that Apollos was:

- A Jew.
- A learned man
- Thoroughly knowledgeable of the Scriptures (AMP: *well versed and mighty in the Scriptures*.).
- Instructed in the way of the Lord.
- A fervent speaker. (Literally (NASB): *fervent in spirit*, Amp: was *burning with spiritual zeal)*

What a combination! His Jewish faith gave him a solid foundation, and he was well educated, particularly in the Scriptures (the Old Testament at that time). Too often I have seen theological study rob someone of their zeal and fervor – but not Apollos. This is the first time we hear of him – but it won't be the last. He became a co-worker of Paul, and played an important role in the development of the church in Corinth. On what appears to be his first missionary journey, the Lord sent him to Ephesus, where he went to the synagogue and boldly spoke about the Messiah. We are told he *taught accurately* about Jesus. This sounds great – but there was a problem.

The danger of limited knowledge

God can powerfully use someone with limited knowledge. He has done so many times. Apollos was a highly educated man, who loved the Scriptures. Many highly educated people may know the Scriptures - but lack full knowledge of the Lord's ways. Many of them are zealous, fervent, and sincere. Nevertheless, they may be sincerely wrong. The church is growing so fast in many areas that there is no time for Bible school – let alone the funds to pay for it. I have noticed an appalling ignorance of church history and the Bible (and how to interpret it) among many church leaders. Perhaps they have a good excuse for their ignorance, yet with such widespread access to the internet and more resources to train leaders than ever before, it seems like there should be many opportunities to learn.

We cannot blame Apollos for what happened in Ephesus. He did his best with what he knew, which was only John's baptism – a baptism of repentance. He did not know about the baptism Jesus had commanded, of identification with his death and resurrection, or the baptism in the Holy Spirit. Perhaps someone came to Alexandria who had listened to Jesus and been baptized by John – but left Jerusalem before Pentecost.

Be teachable

More serious than lack of knowledge is an unteachable spirit: a prideful person who is not open to receiving the truth. Thank God, that was not the case with Apollos. God put a couple in his path to explain the Gospel to him more fully. They took him aside and invited him to their home, where they shared the full Gospel with him. We are desperately in need of people like Priscilla and Aquila today, who have the love, the tenderness, and the willingness to pour into the lives of younger leaders. When someone needs correction, it is always better to take him or her aside. Inviting them to your home shows real care. Public correction usually results in defensiveness, and rarely is effective. Could God use you to more fully explain the ways of the Lord to a young minister? Or you and your wife?

One way the church grew so rapidly in the first century was by sending evangelists to other cities to spread the Gospel. Apollos felt called to Corinth, and the brothers in Ephesus encouraged him on his way. God still calls many to go out on "mission trips." It is important to send someone out with proper recommendation (Emails, or a letter) and to make sure anyone coming to minister in your church comes with the recommendation of a respected pastor or leader.

Put what you learn into practice

Apollos was a fast learner, and was well equipped to prove the truth about Jesus from the Scriptures. We need to study and prepare ourselves to carefully use the Scriptures to defend our message. Sadly, cult group members often seem better equipped to use the Scriptures for their purposes than we are. It is *God's* Word, not yours, which has the power to convict and transform. Though we want to be sensitive, and not belligerent, there are times to publicly refute the errors of other doctrines – and even do it vigorously, as though you really are convinced it is the truth. After all, God needs warriors, not wimps.

Have you known the blessings of receiving someone like Apollos? I pray that you may be of great help to those God would send you to.

Is there some area in which you, like Apollos, may lack knowledge? Are you open to being taught? What can you do to begin to remedy that lack?

Things are about to get exciting in Ephesus. Apollos did his best, but it is Paul's arrival that really got the church going.

2 PAUL'S MINISTRY IN EPHESUS

ACTS 19:1–12

Apollos had laid the foundation for a new church in Ephesus, but several key pieces were missing. God sends another man to fill in those gaps.

Paul arrives in Ephesus

While Apollos was at Corinth, Paul took the road through the interior and arrived at Ephesus. There he found some disciples. (19:1)

Paul apparently had not met Apollos, and was unaware of his ministry there. He did find the fruit of his labors – a small group of disciples. But, oddly, Paul immediately sensed that something was wrong. We already know there was a problem with their baptism, but now we learn of another problem:

² Paul asked them, "Did you receive the Holy Spirit when you believed?" They answered, "No, we have not even heard that there is a Holy Spirit." ³ So Paul asked, "Then what baptism did you receive?" "John's baptism," they replied.

Believers without the Holy Spirit?

The Lord may have revealed it to him, but most likely Paul noticed something lacking among these disciples: There was no power, no manifestations of the Holy Spirit. His expectation was when you believe in Jesus, you receive the Spirit. That was usually the case in Acts. Someone would accept Jesus, be baptized in water, and at the same time be baptized in the Spirit, usually accompanied by speaking in tongues. However, that wasn't always the case, as we see now in Ephesus. Before he could do any further ministry, Paul's first priority was correcting this.

Much controversy has surrounded the baptism in the Holy Spirit. Those without a distinct second experience bristle at the suggestion that they might be lacking something. Paul was not pointing fingers or questioning their spirituality. He knew the fullness of the Spirit was essential for the Christian life, and he would do whatever it took to make sure these disciples received it. Without the Spirit's presence, he could not build a church. Here is a clear biblical case (and not the only one) where sincere believers in Jesus had not received the Spirit. Obviously, for some, it is going to be a second experience. How about you? Did you receive the Holy Spirit when you believed? If you are not sure, are you open to whatever the Lord might do to give you that necessary power?

Here the issue was simple ignorance: They had never even heard there was a Holy Spirit. That is true in some churches, which barely talk about the Spirit. The church I grew up in rarely mentioned Him, and when they did, they called Him the Holy Ghost. I pictured Caspar, some kind of weird ghost figure. Now, as then, some people simply do not know about the Spirit, or His role in our lives.

The connection of water and Spirit baptism

It is important to follow Paul's thinking. When he found out that they did not know about the Spirit, his first thought was, there must have been some problem with their baptism. For Paul there was an intimate connection between water and Spirit baptism. If they had been baptized, they should have the Spirit. However, it is even possible to be baptized – in ignorance – and not receive everything the Lord has for you. They had only been baptized in John's baptism, a baptism of repentance.

⁴ Paul said, "John's baptism was a baptism of repentance. He told the people to believe in the one coming after him, that is, in Jesus." ⁵ On hearing this, they were baptized in the name of the Lord Jesus.

There is biblical support for being baptized again! If you were baptized as a baby, or without really accepting Jesus, you can be baptized a second time.

In the Name of Jesus only?

There is a dangerous doctrine that denies the trinity and says you must be baptized in the name of Jesus only; no other baptism is valid. But Jesus commanded us to baptize in the name of the Father, Son, and Holy Spirit (Matthew 28:19). And Acts 8:15-16 says:

*As soon as [the apostles] arrived, they prayed for these new believers to receive the Holy Spirit. The **Holy Spirit had not yet come upon any of them, for they had only been baptized in the name of the Lord Jesus.***

Here again, with the rapid growth of the church, there had been an error in the way baptism was administered, and it also resulted in believers not receiving the Holy Spirit. What was the error? Baptizing in the name of Jesus only. Acts 19:5 does not give a formula to use in baptism. It is simply telling us that, instead of John's baptism of repentance, the Ephesians were now baptized in identification with Jesus.

Correcting the problem

⁶ When Paul placed his hands on them, the Holy Spirit came on them, and they spoke in tongues and prophesied.

When we follow the New Testament model, we should experience similar results:

1. They were baptized in water.
2. Paul laid hands on them. There is power in the laying on of hands, and God often uses it to impart the Holy Spirit.
3. The Holy Spirit came on them.
4. They spoke in tongues – and prophesied. The coming of the Spirit is almost always accompanied by some kind of proclamation from our mouths: praise, new tongues, and in this case, prophecy (probably more closely resembling the ecstatic prophesying spoken of in the Old Testament than giving prophetic messages).

Has the Spirit come on you? On your church? Has there been evidence of it? Have you been baptized in water? Are there people you need to lay hands on, in faith that God wants to fill them with the Spirit?

The growth of the church

⁷ There were about twelve men in all.

This was a small church, but don't despise the day of small beginnings. What is impressive about this number? With twelve disciples, Jesus changed the world, and God raised up a powerful church in Ephesus from these twelve. The number really is not important; it is the anointing and unity of the brothers that releases God's power. When the Spirit comes, as it did here, you can expect growth. Look at what happened at Pentecost. Your church may not be very big, but don't let that discourage you. Do not be intimidated by mega-churches. Your church will grow, and God will do great things to glorify his name. If for some reason it stubbornly refuses to grow, you may need to evaluate if the Spirit is present in His fullness.

8 Paul entered the synagogue and spoke boldly there for three months, arguing persuasively about the kingdom of God. 9 But some of them became obstinate; they refused to believe and publicly maligned the Way. So Paul left them. He took the disciples with him and had discussions daily in the lecture hall of Tyrannus. 10 This went on for two years, so that all the Jews and Greeks who lived in the province of Asia heard the word of the Lord.

11 God did extraordinary miracles through Paul, 12 so that even handkerchiefs and aprons that had touched him were taken to the sick, and their illnesses were cured and the evil spirits left them.

This is amazing — and serves as a great example of how to plant a church or enter into a new field. Is anything like this happening in your church?

1. **Public proclamation of Jesus Christ**. We go first to people who have some knowledge of the Word, usually

some of them are hungering for the truth. Here Paul started at the synagogue.

2. **Rejection and persecution**. You can count of it! But instead of giving up, they just moved to a school, or lecture hall. Sometimes we need to separate from those who do not accept the truth of the Word.

3. **Boldness**. Paul spoke *boldly*.

4. **Perseverance**. They were there every day – for two years!

5. **Arguing persuasively about the kingdom of God**. How much do you speak about the kingdom? It was a major theme in Jesus' teaching – especially in the Gospel of Matthew. Unfortunately, today we often hear more about men's kingdoms than God's kingdom.

6. **Saturation**. The whole province heard the word. Can you say the same of your city?

7. **Signs and wonders confirming the Word**. God did extraordinary miracles through Paul: Sickness was healed and demons cast out. It was the same in Jesus' ministry and throughout the book of Acts. How about your ministry?

Do you think God could do the same thing today? Do you think He wants to? Why not? God wants to glorify Himself!

Many people are suffering under demonic oppression. Sickness abounds despite the massive amounts we spend on medical care. What do you think would happen if your church became known as a place where people regularly found healing? How about some of the most notorious sinners in your community getting free of their demons and being transformed by the power of Christ?

Preparing for the Four Steps:

The Doctrinal Foundation in Ephesians 1–3

3   CHOSEN, ADOPTED, AND REDEEMED – GUARANTEED!

EPHESIANS 1:1–14

¹Paul, an apostle of Christ Jesus by the will of God,

To the saints who are at Ephesus and who are faithful in Christ Jesus:

² Grace to you and peace from God our Father and the Lord Jesus Christ. (NASB)

Who is present in each phrase of these first two verses? Jesus Christ!

- Jesus sends His servants, the apostles, to establish and supervise churches, which are now present as the Body of Christ in millions of places all over the world. These apostles form the foundation of His church and are given His authority. No one just decides he wants to be an apostle, nor do other leaders in the church choose them. It is only by God's sovereign choice that someone is sent out as an apostle. It is a very serious thing to claim to be an apostle!

- Believers are called "saints" and "faithful." Not like the saints of the Catholic church, but in the sense that every believer is separated from the world to live in holiness. God sanctifies us by His Spirit; then it is our responsibility to walk in holiness and be faithful to our Savior. If we keep sinning, we crucify Christ all over again (Hebrews 6:4-6)! First, we find ourselves *in* Jesus,

23

and *remain* in Him, as He describes in John 15; then He places us in a community to be part of his Body in that place.

- o   God works with a people, with a group of believers. True, the decision to accept Christ is individual, but then God places us in a Body.
- o   How is your experience right now in his Body?
- o   How is your holiness? Would your family say you are a saint?
- o   How is your faithfulness? Of course you are not perfect – but are you faithful to Jesus?

- That Body, that branch, is sustained by the head, the vine: Jesus Christ. It receives everything it needs from the Father and the Son. Together, they minister grace and peace to His church. We experience it on an individual basis, but it is when we are in the vine, as part of his Body, that we can most fully experience His grace and peace. It is God's gift to the Church.

³All praise to God, the Father of our Lord Jesus Christ, who has blessed us with every spiritual blessing in the heavenly realms because we are united with Christ. (NLT)

Every spiritual blessing

No, it is not a misprint, or a bad translation. That is what the Greek says. That is God's Word: *You* already have every possible spiritual blessing. How can that be? Because you are *in* Christ. You are *united* with Him! There are not different levels in the Body of Christ, with some receiving more blessings than others. God is not holding out on some blessings for some future time when you are ready to receive them; He has already blessed us with every blessing.

- These blessings are in the heavenly realms. We are not talking about material things. God really is not interested in that new house, that sports car, or the latest technology. To experience these blessings you have to separate from the world and dwell with Christ in the heavenly realms; your heart has to be in heaven.
- These are spiritual blessings.
- They are experienced in Christ, when you are united with Him and abiding in Him: Following Him, serving Him, and living in His presence.

Praise God! He is worthy of our worship! How can you help but praise Him when He has done so much for you? God is not holding back anything from you.

Chosen

⁴For he chose us in him before the creation of the world to be holy and blameless in his sight.

Many Christians struggle with the doctrine of election. It is hard to reconcile with our free will, which the Scriptures also teach. But why complain? What could be better than God choosing you? The problem is that it can appear that God chooses some and rejects others.

But hold on. Let's look carefully at what the verse actually says. It does not say He chose *me*. Or *you*. He chose *us*. He chooses a people. What God decided before the creation of the world is that this people would be holy and blameless in his sight. We are predestined as the Body of Christ to walk in holiness, free from every stain of sin. It does not say that this election has to do with our salvation. God's prior decision involves the destiny of those who believe: He already decided that we would be holy and blameless. It does not necessarily mean He chooses some and rejects others.

Notice it says *in his sight.* We are not yet perfect yet. We still struggle with sin, but Christ's blood and righteousness cover us.

And there is more to this election.

Adopted children

In love [5] *he predestined us for adoption to sonship through Jesus Christ, in accordance with his pleasure and will—* [6] *to the praise of his glorious grace, which he has freely given us in the One he loves.*

Once again, the predestination is not individual, but corporate. What God decided since the beginning was to have a great family of adopted sons and daughters; those who come to Christ are predestined to be adopted into His family.

If you are an adopted child, you already know something about adoption. If you have adopted a child (or a pet), you are well aware of the deep love of an adoptive parent. It obviously is a great privilege to be adopted into God's family. That alone should be enough to fill our hearts with worship and thanksgiving for the rest of our lives.

Unfortunately, not everyone is a God's child. In the sense that we are His creation, yes, but it is only through Jesus that you can become part of His family. Not through Muhammad or anyone else. Only Jesus. Jesus is His beloved, the Apple of his eye. The Father wants many brothers and sisters for His beloved Son.

What does it mean to you to be God's son? It should be life changing! It should transform your self-image. The Lord of the universe has adopted you!

God has another purpose in adopting us: He wants everyone to marvel at His incredible grace, including us miserable sinners in His family. It is pure grace, a gift. He did not choose you because you were handsome, more spiritual, or better than anyone else was. No, it is His grace. Amazing grace. Amazing love.

If God already predestined our adoption, what can stop it? And once He has adopted you, he is not going to toss you out of His family. Discipline you, yes. But He will not disown you. We still have the freedom to rebel, reject Him, and leave home. But our adoption gives us great security. As a little kid goes running to Daddy's arms, run to your Abba Father. Intercede for your brothers and sisters in his family with faith in what the Word of God says: They are to be holy and without blemish. It is God's will. He has already decided it. They are predestined for it.

Redeemed

[7]In him we have redemption through his blood, the forgiveness of sins, in accordance with the riches of God's grace[8] that he lavished on us with all wisdom and understanding.

There it is again: grace. God knows exactly what He is doing. He doesn't grudgingly give us these blessings. He pours them out in accordance with His riches (unlimited!) and *lavishes* them on us. Literally, it says they are *"made abundant to us."* He has carefully thought this out: He employs all his wisdom and understanding (also unlimited!) in determining exactly how to go all out for us. You do not have to wait for some future time when you have earned it; this outpouring of grace has already occurred. We just have to receive it.

Two very important things that God has done for us are included in this outpouring:

- He redeemed you. God set you free from your bondage to sin, as one would pay the price to set a slave free. You were lost. You could never earn it or get enough money together to buy your freedom. You would be a slave for the rest of your life, but God rescued you.
- He forgave your sins. There is no way you could be good enough to balance out the penalty for your sin. The only just consequence of your rebellion to God is death, but God is very wise. He understands us. He knows that he will be richly compensated for his grace. A great family of redeemed and forgiven humanity will bring Him glory and praise.

Never take these gifts lightly. They come a very high price: the blood and life of Jesus Christ. He paid the price. He bought you. You owe Him your life, your obedience, and your worship.

God's plan for history

[9] God has now revealed to us his mysterious plan regarding Christ, a plan to fulfill his own good pleasure. [10] And this is the plan: At the right time he will bring everything together under the authority of Christ—everything in heaven and on earth. (NLT)

It was a mystery. No one could ever figure it out. A mystery in the Bible is not a "whodunit." It is something we did not know, but which the Spirit has revealed to us.

Satan divides; God unites. The devil brings conflict; Christ bring peace and unity. The enemy encourages rebellion and individualism; Jesus is Lord. He wants to establish a kingdom of joy and peace, where everyone submits to His Lordship.

We don't see this unity yet, not even in the church. We are waiting for the *"right time"* – literally *"the fulfillment of the times"* (AMP: *the climax of the ages*). Many think we are just about at the "right time," but there is certainly a lot left to bring together under Christ's authority. Of course, much of that will have to wait until Christ returns to this earth to vanquish His enemies and establish His kingdom. Right now, there is a huge divide between heaven and earth, but at that time, everything will come together under Christ. I cannot wait!

Much as we might like to, we cannot establish his kingdom by our own efforts. Despite all our prayer and hard work, we will not see everything united under Christ right now. But that is our goal and heart's desire. Anything we can do to advance that objective is great. We want to extend His Lordship to as many areas as we can, and bring as many into his Kingdom as possible. As Francis Schaeffer eloquently stated it, "there is to be substantial healing now in all areas of alienation caused by sin, and total healing at Christ's return."

Heirs

[11]*In Him also we have obtained an inheritance, having been predestined according to His purpose who works all things after the counsel of His will,* [12] *to the end that we who were the first to hope in Christ would be to the praise of His glory.* (NASB)

There it is again: predestined. God has adopted us as sons and daughters. Now, as members of his family, we are also heirs. Don't worry if you were not fortunate enough to have rich ancestors who passed down an inheritance; *God* has an inheritance set apart for you!

God has a plan! You may have had plans. Probably many of them never came to pass. However, you can be sure that everything God purposes works out according to His plan. He has the power and all the necessary resources to make sure of that. Are you familiar with God's plan for history? For your life? For your family? He has a plan! There is a purpose for your life! And when you are living in that plan, you will experience purpose and peace. If you resist His plan, you will find yourself very frustrated.

Are you living "to the praise of his glory?" Do others see Jesus in your life and glorify God for the wonders of his grace displayed in you? Is there something you need to change?

Have you put your hope in Christ? Or are your hopes still centered on your money, education, talents, the government, or some person?

A guarantee

[13] And you also were included in Christ when you heard the message of truth, the gospel of your salvation. When you believed, you were marked in him with a seal, the promised Holy Spirit, [14] who is a deposit guaranteeing our inheritance until the redemption of those who are God's possession—to the praise of his glory.

I hope you sense the great security in what Paul has already written: you are adopted into God's family, given an inheritance, and chosen by God. Now he gives us a guarantee! Yes, there are guarantees in the Bible! Here it is the seal of the Holy Spirit. You are a marked man! Like cattle, there is a spiritual brand on your life. Satan and the entire heavenly host know you belong to Jesus. It is a guarantee of your inheritance.

How do you receive that guarantee? It starts by hearing the Gospel, the message of salvation by faith in Jesus Christ. When you accept that message, believing it to be true, God promises you the Holy Spirit. Again, the Spirit is not for a select group of super-spiritual Christians. It is God's gift, God's promise, to every believer.

We have already been redeemed, bought back from your slavery to sin, but we are still waiting for that final redemption when we are delivered from all the mess in this world. On that day, when Christ establishes his kingdom here on earth, you will receive your inheritance. Once again, God does it for the praise of His glory. He longs for our worship, and these few verses make it abundantly clear that He deserves it.

What a glorious start to this letter! We know God's plan for all of history! We can see how He is calling people and putting them in place as members of His Body to advance His kingdom. Have you accepted Christ? Are you experiencing the benefits of adoption as a child of God? Do you have the seal of the Holy Spirit on your life?

4   CHRIST THE HEAD OVER ALL THINGS

EPHESIANS 1:15–23

Paul just finished describing seven blessings guaranteed by the divine deposit of the Holy Spirit in us. Reflecting on those blessings moves him to pray. He is grateful for what the Ephesians have – but he is still going to ask God for much more. Both are important: We should recognize all that God has already done for us and maintain an attitude of gratitude, but there is always more we can experience.

The importance of your relationship to Christ and other believers

[15] For this reason, ever since I heard about your faith in the Lord Jesus and your love for all God's people, [16] I have not stopped giving thanks for you, remembering you in my prayers.

How do you respond when you hear about God's work in other believers or another church? Do you automatically go to the Lord, thanking Him for the positive things – and interceding for whatever needs you may see? Do you pray continually for a church or Christian brothers you deeply love? How is your prayer life? Paul could not stop praying!

Of all the positive things that Paul knew about this church, the two that most impressed him were:

- Their vertical relationship with God. They have a solid faith in Jesus, which gives Paul the freedom to move on to deeper teaching.
- Their horizontal relationships with other believers. They not only *talk* about love, they *demonstrate* it. The Greek word is *agape*, God's unconditional love. Like their Father, who is no respecter of persons, they have a sincere love for *all* his people.

Notice that Paul does not mention their beautiful building, all the programs in the church, how God had prospered them, or the great worship band. Those things should serve to strengthen and encourage our *relationship* with God and with other believers. If the building and programs take priority, they can become idols. The Christian life is all about relationships, and there will be lots of teaching about them in this letter.

Indeed, one of the most important marks of maturity is the state of our relationships. How is your faith in Christ, your relationship to the Lord? The goal of strong faith is not to claim blessings for ourselves, but to walk with Jesus in faith. How is your love for all God's people? Are there demonstrations of that love? Or is it just talk?

That they may know God better

[17] I keep asking that the God of our Lord Jesus Christ, the glorious Father, may give you the Spirit of wisdom and revelation, so that you may know him better.

It is interesting that Paul would ask God to give them the Spirit, since we know from Acts 19 that the Holy Spirit had gloriously baptized them. But apparently it is possible to receive more, even after that baptism. Ask God to give you more of his Spirit!

There are various facets of the Spirit's work in our lives. Here we learn three things about Him:

1. He is a Spirit of wisdom; the source of the wisdom we need to navigate this complex world.
2. He is a Spirit of revelation. The Spirit manifests in gifts of prophecy and word of knowledge, which reveal God's heart. He also reveals God in the Scriptures. Here, however, I believe Paul is thinking about the revelation of God's character in the heart of each believer.
3. The Spirit helps us know God better. He leads us into all truth and opens the eyes of our hearts. If you want to know God better, ask Him for more of His Spirit, and seek the Spirit's fullness in your daily walk.

Is this the cry of your heart? Is it your first request to God – for you and your loved ones? Do you long to know God better?

The eyes of their hearts enlightened

[18] I pray that the eyes of your heart may be enlightened in order that you may know the hope to which he has called you, the riches of his glorious inheritance in the saints, [19] and his incomparably great power for us who believe.

Paul already spoke of the Ephesians' faith (verse 15), and from what he writes in this letter it is obvious they have been believers for some time. Surely they had heard about heaven, hope, and the power of God! However, you can be in church for years and hear God's Word every Sunday – and never grasp the depths of our faith. Some things are only received through revelation. Paul intercedes for enlightenment in three areas that will transform your daily life:

1. The hope to which God has called us. In 1 Corinthians, Paul wrote that faith, hope, and love are most important. He has already touched on each of them in this letter. Our hope is eternal life in God's kingdom. We know there has to be more to this life than what we experience here on earth. The Spirit shows us some of what awaits us, and makes what can be a dry doctrine into a living, certain, hope, which shapes our daily lives.

2. The riches of his glorious inheritance in the saints. This inheritance could be taken two ways:

    a. We are God's inheritance. Paul gives the church a very exalted position in this letter. It is very possible that God would see us as His rich heritage. To realize that should do wonders for our self-image. It is amazing that the King of glory would delight in you and me as His inheritance! Most people hope for an inheritance of money, land, or houses. God could have the whole universe, but He has chosen us for His inheritance. So what kind of inheritance should you be thinking about? Maybe those people that you have brought to Jesus and discipled?

    b. It could also mean the inheritance we will receive as God's adopted children, which Paul already mentioned in verse 14. It is amazing to contemplate the riches awaiting us in the future. It should help us endure the trials of this life!

3. His incomparably great power for us who believe. Some would say it means that if you believe more, if you have more faith, you will receive more power. However, I believe that "us who believe" means every Christian.

Paul said in verse three that we already have every spiritual blessing: Every believer has access to the same power. Based on my observations of the prayers and lifestyle of the majority of Christians, I would say that very few understand that power.

Have you ever been praying for something and God's presence so fills your heart that you just start praising Him? It looks like that happened to Paul. Petitions were put aside as the glories of Christ filled his thoughts.

Just how great is that power?

[19]*That power is the same as the mighty strength* [20]*he exerted when he raised Christ from the dead and seated him at his right hand in the heavenly realms,* [21]*far above all rule and authority, power and dominion, and every name that is invoked, not only in the present age but also in the one to come.*

There is no greater power than giving life to a dead man, and the working of that power in Christ did not end with the resurrection. In fact, it just began there:

- The Father seated Christ at His right hand in the heavenly realms. It is interesting that Paul did not say "in heaven." He spoke in verse three of the blessings we have in the heavenly realms. We tend to think of heaven as a fixed place, but it probably encompasses the entire spiritual realm apart from the physical world we know.
- Christ is seated at the Father's right hand, a position of great authority. He is not talking of a literal seat, but of what we understand to be the position of highest privilege and authority.

- Christ is above every rule and authority, power and dominion. Whatever power exists in heaven or on earth, Jesus is above it. Kings, demons, or any other entity.
- Christ is above every name – whether it be Muhammad or any other god or spiritual leader.
- There are powers in this world, and others in the world to come. Christ is over all of them.

This same Christ is your Savior! Your Lawyer! Your Redeemer! Your High Priest! Your older brother! Your friend! Christ – and all his power – is for you! And we have access to that power through prayer.

Christ the Head of all things

[22] God has put all things under the authority of Christ and has made him head over all things for the benefit of the church. [23] And the church is his body; it is made full and complete by Christ, who fills all things everywhere with himself.

We saw God's plan in verse ten: to unite everything in heaven and earth under Christ. Now Paul is going to finish what started as a prayer (but turned out being a doxology to the greatness of Christ) with a revelation of Christ's current work:

1. God already has placed *everything* under Christ's authority. It may not look that way, but Jesus already has all power and dominion. That should give us great faith as we pray to extend his kingdom.
2. Christ is the head of everything.
3. He functions in that capacity primarily for the up building of the church. Ultimately, all the power and authority that Christ exercises is for the benefit of the church.

4. The church *is* the Body of Christ; not just a metaphor – in reality it *is* His body.
5. The church is the fullness of Christ. It is not only made full and complete by Christ; it *is His fullness*. No other expression of Christ in the world today is more important. You cannot separate Christ from his church. Those who claim to love Christ and want to follow Him, but do not want anything to do with the church, are deceived. Christ's fullness is only found in the church.
6. Christ fills all things everywhere with His presence. That presence keeps the universe working. In Him we live, and move, and have our being (Acts 17:28). Seek Christ's presence and fullness in all of your life!

If the church is this important to God, it makes sense that Satan will do everything possible to destroy it, and, especially, to keep believers away from the Body of Christ.

Is Christ your head? The head of your family? Of your church? Are you submitted to His authority? Are you experiencing his presence as part of His Body, in a healthy church?

5   God fulfills his plan:

Reconciliation with God
Ephesians 2:1–10

The first chapter of Ephesians gave us a glorious vision of our blessings in Christ. We saw God's amazing power, which is available to us. The church, the Body of Christ, is the fullness of God's Son. The major themes of the letter – particularly our relationships with God and others – have been introduced. Now Paul steps back a bit to remind us of who we were, and how God has changed us. With all the blessings as God's adopted children, we might be tempted to think we are special, and fall prey to boastful pride. Understandably, the person God has rescued from a life of sin often wants to forget about his past life. Sadly, he can become a Pharisee, looking down on someone still caught in sin. To stay humble, sometimes it is good to remember where we came from.

We were all dead

The first three verses of this chapter, essentially a condensation of the first three chapters of Romans, describe the human condition.

¹As for you, you were dead in your transgressions and sins.

And you [He made alive when you] were [spiritually] dead and separated from Him because of your transgressions and sins. (AMP)

Without Christ, we are dead. There is no way we can save or help ourselves. We all start there. We are all sinners, no matter which sin. We are all dead. The cause of death is irrelevant. Every dead person is the same: No life, no hope, nothing.

Transgressions probably refer to deliberate sins of commission; conscious violations of what we know is right. *Sins* refer to sins of omission: we simply fail to live up to God's standards. The root of our problem is rebellion and disobedience. By nature, we want to do things our own way. We resist authority. Every day we make decisions to ignore what we know is right.

But there is another dynamic that contributes to our death.

The prince of the power of the air

² in which you used to live when you followed the ways of this world and of the ruler of the kingdom of the air, the spirit who is now at work in those who are disobedient.

in which you once walked. You were following the ways of this world [influenced by this present age], in accordance with the prince of the power of the air (Satan), the spirit who is now at work in the disobedient [the unbelieving, who fight against the purposes of God]. (AMP)

Several times in these verses Paul emphasizes the fact that we are all the same; no one is better than anyone else is. Whether you are a successful politician, businessman, or street criminal, we all served the devil. We all had corrupt hearts. Sin is sin. Often it is harder for the "respectable" person to admit his need for salvation, while the addict realizes he needs a Savior.

We all lived and walked in the world, and that system, with its corrupt values, contributes to our problem. It is part of the trinity we battle: the world, the flesh, and the devil. Today the world is more corrupt than ever. The media – especially TV and the internet - have enormous influence, and it is largely ungodly. Unfortunately, most Christians pass far more time in front of those screens than in front of their Bibles.

You might remember the comedian Flip Wilson, who popularized the saying "the devil made me do it." It is easy to blame the devil for our sin and rebellion, but we must take responsibility for our own decisions. Some make fun of the Christian who is always talking about the devil, but the truth is that if you are not under the Lordship of Christ, you are under the power of the evil one. It is wise to remember that as we relate to unsaved coworkers and family members. To plunder the enemy's house we must first bind the strong man (Matthew 12:29).

So what does this verse teach us?

- The devil is a spirit. There is a great army of demons in an invisible, spiritual world, and the devil is their leader.

- Most are not even aware of it, but without Christ, people naturally obey the thoughts and desires the devil sows in their hearts. We follow the ways of this world. Few people consciously want to serve the devil, but Satan is very clever, masquerading as an angel of light.

- The devil *is now at work in those who are disobedient.* We assume that they are not Christians, but a believer who disobeys God opens his heart to the devil and possible enemy strongholds.

The flesh

³ *All of us also lived among them at one time, gratifying the cravings of our flesh and following its desires and thoughts. Like the rest, we were by nature deserving of wrath.*

Among these [unbelievers] we all once lived in the passions of our flesh [our behavior governed by the sinful self], indulging the desires of human nature [without the Holy Spirit] and [the impulses] of the [sinful] mind. We were, by nature, children [under the sentence] of [God's] wrath, just like the rest [of mankind]. (AMP)

Now Paul changes his focus. Yes, it is true that the devil works in the rebel heart, but there are also two powerful forces at work in every human being. They are manifestations of our flesh:

- Our passions and desires. We all know that struggle. Most people in the world, without giving it a second thought, do whatever they feel like. There are healthy, God-given passions and desires. The problem is when they control us, instead of us having self-control.

- Our fallen nature. Sin entered our race when Adam and Eve disobeyed God, and that rebellion has plagued us ever since. We are born with a sinful nature: Self is the center of the universe. It is *our* will that is important and *our* purposes that have priority.

The whole race has received a death sentence. Apart from God's grace and salvation, we are objects of His wrath. The situation is bad, and there is no apparent way out.

The big "but"

⁴ But because of his great love for us, God, who is rich in mercy, ⁵ made us alive with Christ even when we were dead in transgressions—it is by grace you have been saved.

But God, being [so very] rich in mercy, because of His great and wonderful love with which He loved us, ⁵ even when we were [spiritually] dead and separated from Him because of our sins, He made us [spiritually] alive together with Christ (for by His grace—His undeserved favor and mercy—you have been saved from God's judgment). (AMP)

A dead man is powerless. Without God's intervention, we would be lost and condemned to an eternal punishment. Everything changed when Christ died on the cross and the Father raised Him from the dead. God took the initiative and did what was necessary to rescue us and save us. But why would He do that?

- He is rich in mercy.

- He loves us.

- He is the one who originally gave us life. Now, just as He gave new life to His Son, He wants to give new life to all His sons and daughters.

- He is a God of grace.

- He is kind and good (verse 7).

United with Christ

⁶ And God raised us up with Christ and seated us with him in the heavenly realms in Christ Jesus.

For he raised us from the dead along with Christ and seated us with him in the heavenly realms because we are united with Christ Jesus. (NLT)

Here it is for the first time, and it is repeated in verse 7: We are *in* Christ Jesus, united with Him. That is amazing! He has barely finished describing our ugly rebellion and sin, and here is God, going to the extreme. He does the most radical thing possible: allow us to share all of life with His Son!

- He raised us from the dead *along with* Jesus.

- He seated us *with* Him in the heavenly realms.

- We are united *with* Christ.

Can you grasp what a great privilege it is to be seated with Christ? What does being united with Christ imply? It doesn't say it here, but we die with Christ, crucifying our flesh. That death is symbolized in baptism, as is our resurrection when we rise from the waters. Baptism is so powerful because it is a symbol of our union with Christ. It would be great simply to be united with Christ in His new life, but we are also seated with Him on heavenly thrones. Way beyond mere belief (demons also believe in Jesus), and even beyond a relationship, we are now *united* to Christ.

Examples of God's grace

7 In order that in the coming ages he might show the incomparable riches of his grace, expressed in his kindness to us in Christ Jesus.

[And He did this] so that in the ages to come He might [clearly] show the immeasurable and unsurpassed riches of His grace in [His] kindness toward us in Christ Jesus [by providing for our redemption]. (AMP)

So God can point to us in all future ages as examples of the incredible wealth of his grace and kindness toward us, as shown in all he has done for us who are united with Christ Jesus. (NLT)

We already saw it in 1:6 & 12: God desperately wants all the principalities and powers (and any humans who will pay attention) to see His incredible grace and kindness. In the future, God is going to proudly present us as examples of that grace. If that is so important to God, it makes sense that He will do everything divinely possible (which is limitless!) to present a good example. He is going to make us look like Jesus. But why wait for the coming ages? Maybe to include as many people as possible, or for the chance to finish the good work He began in us.

Saved by grace through faith

⁸ For it is by grace you have been saved, through faith—and this is not from yourselves, it is the gift of God— ⁹ not by works, so that no one can boast.

For it is by grace [God's remarkable compassion and favor drawing you to Christ] that you have been saved [actually delivered from judgment and given eternal life] through faith. And this [salvation] is not of yourselves [not through your own effort], but it is the [undeserved, gracious] gift of God; ⁹ not as a result of [your] works [nor your attempts to keep the Law], so that no one will [be able to] boast or take credit in any way [for his salvation]. (AMP)

God saved you by his grace when you believed. And you can't take credit for this; it is a gift from God. ⁹ Salvation is not a reward for the good things we have done, so none of us can boast about it. (NLT)

Once again, Paul wants to make very clear that all these blessings have nothing to do with our merits. The contrast between what we were, and the new life God gives us, is amazing! And it is all by grace! God wants it that way, so no one can claim any part in their salvation. Once again, we are all the same: Dead and condemned to hell. The only thing we can do is believe what we hear in the good news of salvation.

- God saved us by His grace.

- We don't deserve it.

- It is God's gift.

- It is not some kind of reward for our good deeds, because no one has enough to balance out our sin.

Created for good works

10 For we are God's handiwork, created in Christ Jesus to do good works, which God prepared in advance for us to do.

For we are His workmanship [His own master work, a work of art], created in Christ Jesus [reborn from above—spiritually transformed, renewed, ready to be used] for good works, which God prepared [for us] beforehand [taking paths which He set], so that we would walk in them [living the good life which He prearranged and made ready for us]. (AMP)

For we are God's masterpiece. He has created us anew in Christ Jesus, so we can do the good things he planned for us long ago. (NLT)

God has another purpose in saving us, aside from providing examples that will bring Him much praise. In the first chapter we saw several things God prepared in the past for us, that are predestined for us. Now we see He also has good works prearranged and made ready for us, and He shapes us specifically to do them. He is hard at work on us, and He knows exactly what He is doing. Everything He does is first class. You and I are God's masterpieces, more impressive than the most awesome things in nature. God originally made us in His image; now He lovingly restores that image when we accept Christ. We are His workmanship (not your wife's workmanship, or your pastor's workmanship). He starts all over with each one of us, creating us anew.

At the beginning of this chapter, we were walking and living in death: depraved, hopeless, and helpless. But God stepped in, and now we are walking in good works!

What does God want to say to you?

- Do you know what good works God has prepared for you? Are you walking in them?

- Are you saved? Have you experienced God's grace, and by simple faith accepted His gift of salvation?

- Are you living in Christ? In union with Him? Do you honestly have any idea what it means to be united to Him? Could you say that it is your experience?

- How much influence does your flesh (with its passions and desires), the world, and the devil have on your daily life? How would say it compares with the influence of God's Word and Spirit?

6 GOD FULFILLS HIS PLAN:

RECONCILIATION WITH OTHERS
EPHESIANS 2:11–22

God has a plan for all history: Jesus as the center of the universe, and everything united in Him. You are part of that plan, if you have been reconciled with God and united with Christ. Your new life starts with salvation, which Paul described in the first part of this chapter. Once our relationship with God has been restored, He can deal with our alienation from others, restoring relationships in families, churches, and society.

In the first century, reconciliation began by abolishing the wall of separation between Jews and Gentiles, a wall constructed by the Jews themselves. They called anyone who was not Jewish a Gentile, with the obvious implication of inferiority. Yet God never intended for this dividing wall. His desire from the beginning was to use Israel as an example to draw others into His kingdom.

As is often the case, pride perpetuated the alienation. Jewish pride focused on a rather odd distinction: circumcision. Paul was very familiar with the prejudice and persecution that pride can produce, and he repeatedly fought to keep this wall of separation broken down. Even among Christians, there is a prideful, sinful, tendency to erect walls! Although Paul points to Jewish pride, Gentiles also need to beware of spiritual pride. Remembering where we came from should keep us humble.

Do not forget where you came from

[11] Don't forget that you Gentiles used to be outsiders. You were called "uncircumcised heathens" by the Jews, who were proud of their circumcision, even though it affected only their bodies and not their hearts. (NLT)

Therefore, remember that formerly you who are Gentiles by birth and called "uncircumcised" by those who call themselves "the circumcision" (which is done in the body by human hands)—

The temple Jesus and Paul knew had three courtyards: for priests, Jewish men, and women. To reach the court of the Gentiles you had to go down 19 steps, where a wall kept them separate. Signs posted on the wall warned of execution for anyone passing it. Two of those signs (in Greek) were found, one in 1871, and one in 1938. Gentiles could see the temple, but could never enter it. Physically, they were excluded.

Circumcision was the defining mark of separation. Although it was God's idea (an interesting study in itself!), like much of Jewish religion, it was external. Their temptation, as seen in Jesus' interaction with the Pharisees, was to focus on appearances, and ignore the soul and spirit.

While Gentiles (most of us) might be quick to point out the hypocrisy, we must remember that it is only by God's grace that we are included in his kingdom. And we must carefully guard ourselves from a sin and plague that has affected the church through the centuries: anti-Semitism. Beware of spiritual pride! We should all stand humbled before God by our unworthiness, and His great love.

Completely lost

[12] In those days you were living apart from Christ. You were excluded from citizenship among the people of Israel, and you did not know the covenant promises God had made to them. You lived in this world without God and without hope. (NLT)

Remember that at that time you were separate from Christ, excluded from citizenship in Israel and foreigners to the covenants of the promise, without hope and without God in the world.

Religion may have been largely external for many Jews, but at least they were part of God's chosen people; they had His word and promises, and participated in His covenants. It was similar to the Christian heritage that the United States had, with the influence of Biblical values on the nation's morals and laws.

These pagans, or Gentiles, lacked any knowledge of God. They had nothing:

- They lived separated from Christ.
- They were excluded from citizenship in Israel.
- They did not know God's promises.
- They were not part of the covenants God made with Israel.
- They lived in this world without God.
- They lived without hope.

In other words, they were completely lost. You do not have to be a Gentile, or a first-century pagan, to feel excluded, different, or hopeless. Unfortunately, there is much alienation and loneliness, even in the Body of Christ. You may have experienced it. God wants to draw you into His family and give you new hope.

The situation looked grim for the Gentiles, but again there was a big "but" that completely changed their lives.

United with Jesus

[13] But now you have been united with Christ Jesus. Once you were far away from God, but now you have been brought near to him through the blood of Christ. (NLT)

But now in Christ Jesus you who once were far away have been brought nearby the blood of Christ.

Praise God! We are no longer far from God! We are close! Like the old saying goes: If God seems far away, guess who moved?

The change starts as union with Christ, described in the first part of the chapter. We are not only *close* to God; we are *united* with Christ. Through His shed blood, Jesus redeemed us, justified us, and forgave our sins. The Jews offered animal sacrifices, but their blood could never unite them with God. Our union is not intellectual, philosophical, political, or military: It is spiritual. Any effort to foster unity must start there.

Jesus is our peace

[14]For he himself is our peace, who has made the two groups one and has destroyed the barrier, the dividing wall of hostility

Before, a dividing wall of hostility separated Gentiles from God and his chosen people. The temple wall was still there when Paul wrote this letter (it was destroyed along with the temple in AD 70). Spiritually, it had been broken down when Jesus died, but sometimes we have to wait for the physical manifestation of something that has already happened in the spirit.

Whether it is peace between Jew and Gentile, peace in a church, or peace in a family, peace is found in a person: Jesus

Christ. When we are united to Christ and focused on Him, we should experience peace with others who are enjoying that same union. If not, we may need to examine the state of that relationship with Christ.

There is no longer Jew, Greek, or any other ethnic group in Christ: We are all one body. That is not to say that those who speak the same language should not worship together, or that there is never a place for a messianic Jewish congregation, but we must be very careful not to erect walls of separation and create divisions.

The real test of our love is not in the church, but with people who are very different from us. Paul may have been thinking of Jesus' teaching:

> *"You have heard that it was said, 'Love your neighbor and hate your enemy.' But I tell you, love your enemies and pray for those who persecute you, that you may be children of your Father in heaven. He causes his sun to rise on the evil and the good, and sends rain on the righteous and the unrighteous. If you love those who love you, what reward will you get? Are not even the tax collectors doing that? And if you greet only your own people, what are you doing more than others? Do not even pagans do that?* (Matthew 5:43-47)

So what place does the law have today?

15 He did this by ending the system of law with its commandments and regulations. He made peace between Jews and Gentiles by creating in himself one new people from the two groups. (NLT)

By setting aside in his flesh the law with its commands and regulations, His purpose was to create in himself one new humanity out of the two, thus making peace.

Here is the answer to a question that many Christians have — especially messianic Jews and Adventists: What part does the law play in the Christian life? Jesus ended the system of laws of commandments and regulations; He abolished it in his flesh when He died on the cross. That is not to say that Old Testament laws do not reveal God's will for our lives. But the *system* of laws was abolished; the *system* of sacrifices and ceremonies under the Old Covenant. Also abolished was the old way of finding peace with God by observing His laws. Paul already wrote in the first part of this chapter that it is not by works, but by faith and the grace of God, that we are saved. Christ abolished the condemnation of a law that required perfect obedience to be accepted by God.

Once again, Paul repeats that Christ made peace between Jew and Gentile. Jesus created something totally new in Himself: a new humanity, a new people, a new race. Paul describes the unity of this new humanity in other Scriptures:

> *Here there is no Gentile or Jew, circumcised or uncircumcised, barbarian, Scythian, slave or free, but Christ is all, and is in all.* (Colossians 3:11)

> *There is neither Jew nor Gentile, neither slave nor free, nor is there male and female, for you are all one in Christ Jesus.* (Galatians 3:28)

Not that those distinctions no longer exist. For example, other passages clearly describe the distinct functions of men and women. Nevertheless, in Christ, we are all equal, and we are all one.

Hostility put to death

¹⁶ *Together as one body, Christ reconciled both groups to God by means of his death on the cross, and our hostility toward each other was put to death.* (NLT)

and in one body to reconcile both of them to God through the cross, by which he put to death their hostility.

The third time! When the Bible repeats something three times, it is because it is very important! The hostility at that time was between Jew and Gentile, but today that can apply to any group that confesses Christ but remains separate, whether from pride, or for cultural reasons. We make light of Christ's work on the cross if we do not pursue reconciliation between everyone who confesses Christ as Lord. We have to do everything possible to be one Body! How grieved Jesus must be over all the divisions in the church!

Even more important than the hostility between ethnic groups, there existed (and still exists for unbelievers) hostility between God and us.

Preach this message of peace!

¹⁷ *He brought this Good News of peace to you Gentiles who were far away from him, and peace to the Jews who were near.* (NLT)

He came and preached peace to you who were far away and peace to those who were near.

It is the same message for everyone: Jesus, and peace with God through Him. That was the message of Christ and the apostles. Our world needs that message of peace! Are you bringing this

Good News to those who are far from you (in other cultures or places), and those who are near (your family, friends, and coworkers)?

Free access to the Father

[18] Now all of us can come to the Father through the same Holy Spirit because of what Christ has done for us. (NLT)

For through him we both have access to the Father by one Spirit.

Before, it was nearly impossible even for Jews to gain access to God, but Christ opened the way for everyone to enter directly into the Father's presence. We all have the same access, and we all have the same Spirit. You do not need a priest to speak to God. Are you taking advantage of this great privilege?

Here we clearly see the Trinity! Because of what the *Son* did, the *Holy Spirit* dwells in us, and ushers us into the presence of the *Father*. The Spirit teaches us how to pray, helps us in our weakness, and unites us.

Members of God's family

[19] So now you Gentiles are no longer strangers and foreigners. You are citizens along with all of God's holy people. You are members of God's family. (NLT)

Consequently, you are no longer foreigners and strangers, but fellow citizens with God's people and also members of his household

Paul spoke of our adoption in chapter one. Now, in summary, he affirms that Gentiles are also citizens in God's kingdom, and are adopted children in His family. We are one big family that meets in various "houses" of worship. We must do everything possible to maintain the unity with other "houses" that are part of God's holy people.

Before you are a citizen of some nation (which also is important), you are a citizen of heaven, of God's kingdom. And before you are part of an earthly family (something precious to us), you are a member of God's family. That is why we call each other "brother" and "sister."

There may be times when you feel like a foreigner or stranger to your own culture, country, or family. It is an uncomfortable feeling, but it is normal for the Christian. Actually, there is more cause for concern if you feel too comfortable in this world.

We are God's house

[20] *Together, we are his house, built on the foundation of the apostles and the prophets. And the cornerstone is Christ Jesus himself.* (NLT)

Paul already said in 1:23 that we *are* the Body of Christ. Now he introduces another metaphor: A house. I just said that we worship in various houses; perhaps it would be more accurate to say in various rooms in the same house, because all believers together comprise Jesus' house. The foundation of that house is the teaching and work of the Apostles (in the New Testament) and the prophets (Old and New Testaments). It may include present day apostles and prophets, but the foundation never changes: It is always the teaching of the Bible.

Jesus is the center of this house, the corner stone. If Christ does not have that key place in a church, or if it does not follow the apostles' teaching as found in the New Testament, it is not part of his house. We must be careful not to make a man or a doctrine the corner stone of a church. It happens only too often.

We are becoming a holy temple

²¹ *We are carefully joined together in him, becoming a holy temple for the Lord.* (NLT)

In him the whole building is joined together and rises to become a holy temple in the Lord.

Now Paul goes a step further in describing the church: we are a holy temple. What an amazing image! What an incredibly exalted vision of the church! But who is joining us together? Do you sense believers around the world rising together to become this glorious temple? Who is designing it and overseeing its construction? The architects and contractors must be Jesus himself, and the Holy Spirit. This might be the most important building project in all of history! Read the detailed biblical instructions for the construction of the tabernacle and the temples! Those buildings are long gone – but this is a lasting temple. It must be extremely well built to survive the devil's attacks.

Peter also describes this house:

> *As you come to him, the living Stone—rejected by humans but chosen by God and precious to him— you also, like living stones, are being built into a spiritual house to be a holy priesthood, offering spiritual sacrifices acceptable to God through Jesus Christ.* (1 Peter 2:4-5)

Unfortunately, the temple I see rising is not very pretty. It seems haphazard, with a wild assortment of designs. Each group seems to be making its own plan, doing its own thing, and paying scant attention to what others are doing. Instead of helping each other, they try to outdo each other in making their part most impressive. It is hard to figure out what happened to the contractor, Jesus Christ! This temple should be a showplace of unity and outstanding construction. People should be drawn to its overwhelming beauty. Christ dwells in this holy temple. It must be worthy of our Savior. I have to confess I am bewildered at why he allows it to look so shabby. But then, I'm not Jesus. I just need to do my part.

Remember, this is a spiritual temple. That is where our focus should be. Is it at the top of our agendas? Have there been gatherings of Christian leaders to discuss what this is all about – and how to best go about building it? Do we even believe this is reality? Or are these just flowery words that Paul used?

We must be careful not to put too much emphasis on buildings. It is not a sin to construct a beautiful building to worship in, but it can easily become an idol, consuming tremendous energy and money. Christ never even *mentioned* building great houses or temples for His family.

²² *And in him you too are being built together to become a dwelling in which God lives by his Spirit.*

The *shekinah* glory that filled the temple in Jerusalem now is manifest when God's family gathers to worship Him. God dwells in this temple. His Spirit fills it. But if the temple is not clean, if there is discord in it, the Spirit will not dwell there. That may explain the absence of the Spirit's power in many churches. If this is to be an adequate dwelling for God, we must be built together, with each living stone in its place. I do not see much emphasis on that in most churches. Do you feel that you are being knit together with other believers in your congregation?

Can you grasp how radical the vision and reality of this new community in Christ really is? It is the context for everything Jesus wants to do in us.

7 HOW GOD FULFILLS HIS PLAN:

THE CHURCH "EVANGELIZES" THE HEAVENLY POWERS

EPHESIANS 3:1–13

¹For this reason I, Paul, the prisoner of Christ Jesus for the sake of you Gentiles—

For this reason [because I preach that you and believing Jews are joint heirs] I, Paul, am the prisoner of Christ Jesus on behalf of you Gentiles— (AMP)

In two short chapters, Paul has given us much to think about. Most important is God's plan to include the Gentiles in His Kingdom. Paul's dedication to the Gentiles landed him in jail. His calling consistently got him in trouble. The Jews were furious with him, jealous to the point of attempting to kill him so they could silence him (see Acts 21:27-36). He went all the way to Jerusalem - and head to head with Peter - to fight for the inclusion of the Gentiles (see Acts 15 and Galatians 2:11-13). If he had not, Jesus could very well have ended up being one more rabbi or prophet in a Jewish sect.

Paul's ministry

² Surely you have heard about the administration of God's grace that was given to me for you, ³ that is, the mystery made known to me by revelation, as I have already written briefly. ⁴ In reading this, then, you will be able to understand my insight into the mystery of Christ, ⁵ which was not made known to people in other generations as it has now been revealed by the Spirit to God's holy apostles and prophets.

We do not know anything about this earlier letter, but it is clear that Paul's encounter with Jesus on the Damascus road, and the revelation he received there, shaped his entire life.

What Paul refers to in verse two can apply to anyone ministering in another culture, any missionary. God gave Paul special grace to establish relationships and start churches among the Gentiles. Everyone knew Paul was a Jew – even a Pharisee. But in obedience to God, he directed his ministry to another group, and God gave him the grace to be accepted by them and communicate to them. That is a grace which God still gives to someone called to another culture or language. It was Paul's responsibility to administer this grace for the benefit of the churches and the Kingdom of God.

Once again, Paul places the apostles and prophets in a special position. Through the Holy Spirit, they receive revelation about God's plans. There is no further "mystery" to be revealed today, but God still reveals His plans to the apostles and prophets of the church. Almost every ministry starts with a revelation of God's plan for a city or group of people.

God's plan

⁶ This mystery is that through the gospel the Gentiles are heirs together with Israel, members together of one body, and sharers together in the promise in Christ Jesus. ⁷ I became a servant of this gospel by the gift of God's grace given me through the working of his power.

⁶ And this is God's plan: Both Gentiles and Jews who believe the Good News share equally in the riches inherited by God's children. Both are part of the same body, and both enjoy the promise of blessings because they belong to Christ Jesus. [7] By God's grace and mighty power, I have been given the privilege of serving him by spreading this Good News. (NLT)

Paul repeats what he shared in chapter two, using three words to describe the position the Gentiles now hold:

- *Heirs*: As God's adopted children, we all share a rich inheritance together.
- *Members* of one body: There is not a Jewish church and a Gentile church. God is not interested in the labels we give churches. We are all members of the same Body of Christ.
- *Sharers*: We all enjoy the same blessings promised in Jesus Christ.

This is God's plan: To establish one unified body from every nation, enjoying all the privileges and blessings of His children. The Holy Spirit revealed this plan to Paul. A commission usually accompanies a revelation; someone is sent to make the revelation reality. Paul became a servant of this Gospel by the gift of God's grace. It is great to study and prepare yourself for ministry, but it is God's call, grace, and gifting that enable you to serve him. A ministry without God's grace and mighty power will be all human effort. There seem to be many in ministry who have never received that revelation of God's call, and are not ministering in His grace or power. You know them by their fruits.

Incomprehensible Riches

[8] Though I am the least deserving of all God's people, he graciously gave me the privilege of telling the Gentiles about the endless treasures available to them in Christ. [9] I was chosen to

explain to everyone this mysterious plan that God, the Creator of all things, had kept secret from the beginning. (NLT)

Paul still felt ashamed of the way he had persecuted the church. He would never forget Stephen's face as he was stoned – the first Christian martyr (Acts 8 & 9:1). Paul considered himself less than the least of God's people, which made the privilege of bringing the Good News to the Gentiles all the more precious.

As with many who are called to an unusual ministry, Paul not only ministered to the Gentiles, he also had to explain what he was doing to everyone else - especially the Jews. That was the hardest part of his calling!

He adds that God is the Creator of all things. Obviously, that gives Him the right to create a new people in Christ, which includes the Gentiles. The riches available to that new creation are incomprehensible and boundless:

- Resurrection from the dead.
- Forgiveness of sins.
- Thrones, on which we are seated with Christ.
- Reconciliation with God.
- Participation in a new community.
- The end of hostility, and enduring peace.
- Access to the Father through the Spirit and the Son.
- A rich inheritance.

Are you enjoying these incredible treasures? Are you aware of all that has been given you in Christ?

Witnesses to rulers in heavenly places

[10] *His intent was that now, through the church, the manifold wisdom of God should be made known to the rulers and*

authorities in the heavenly realms, [11] according to his eternal purpose that he accomplished in Christ Jesus our Lord.

[10] *God's purpose in all this was to use the church to display his wisdom in its rich variety to all the unseen rulers and authorities in the heavenly places. [11] This was his eternal plan, which he carried out through Christ Jesus our Lord.* (NLT)

God's plan for the church goes way beyond:

- Uplifting and anointed worship services.
- Warm fellowship.
- Good teaching on how to experience God's blessings.
- Internet, radio and TV programs.
- Beautiful buildings.

Yes, God wants the church to demonstrate His love and power to the world. He wants to heal, save, and affect all society with Kingdom values, but His plan for the church goes way beyond this world: It reaches to the heavenly realms. There are rulers and authorities in heavenly places that are still unconvinced of God's infinite power and wisdom. And yes, although it may seem incredible, God has chosen us, His church, to display His character and wisdom. It is one thing for God to show off the glories of heaven and talk about all He has done, but we are the proof that it really works. This new community, which includes all races and cultures and classes, is unique. The love and unity we demonstrate, in spite of our differences, is a powerful testimony to God's miracle in our lives.

God does not use angels to evangelize the world; He uses us. We are called to testify to our families, co-workers – everyone! – about who God is and what He has done for us. I am afraid we are not doing that very well. But even more serious is our failure to evangelize the authorities we cannot even see! That is a great privilege – and responsibility, a responsibility few seem to be aware of. Apparently, these heavenly rulers are watching to see what God can do. They want to know if it is just talk: Is the church going to fail like Israel did? Unfortunately, they may have the wrong impression about God from what they have seen in the church. How can we dishonor the One who gave His life for us? Do you want Jesus to be a laughingstock before the principalities and powers, because it seems like He died in vain? As good sons who love our Father, aren't we obliged to do everything possible to honor this call, and give them the best witness possible of God's love, grace, goodness, and power?

Free Access to God's Presence

[12] Because of Christ and our faith in him, we can now come boldly and confidently into God's presence. [13] So please don't lose heart because of my trials here. I am suffering for you, so you should feel honored. (NLT)

[12] In him and through faith in him we may approach God with freedom and confidence. [13] I ask you, therefore, not to be discouraged because of my sufferings for you, which are your glory.

At first, we might get the impression that Paul is not a very good witness to those principalities: He is suffering because he obeyed his call! He is in jail! He could have had a comfortable life as a Pharisee! But God helps us in the trials and comforts us in tribulation – and that is a powerful witness. Those heavenly authorities see God's supernatural power at work in Paul, as he continued ministering and rejoicing despite the persecution.

Paul points to one of the most impressive privileges we have as Christians: Through your faith in Jesus and his Word, you can enter His presence with full boldness and confidence. You cannot see it, and you may not feel anything. It is all about faith. In spite of the devil's attacks, we are secure in Christ. We dwell with Christ in heavenly places! Paul took advantage of that privilege every day.

The church is God's plan

Paul has revealed the focus of God's plan for this age: one united Body of Christ. This is the mystery that was so fiercely resisted by the Jews. There are not two parallel plans: one for Israel, and the other for believers in the Jewish Messiah. There are not two covenants: The covenants of the Old Testament have taken a giant leap forward in the New Covenant in Jesus Christ. Far from being what some call "Replacement Theology," this is a theology of fulfillment, a huge expansion of God's saving work. No longer is God's plan focused on one family in a tiny plot of land in the mid-east. It is not about one nation displaying God's greatness. The promised Davidic king has come, and His name is Jesus. He does not rule in a palace in Jerusalem, but from the heavenly throne room of God Almighty, at the right hand of his Father. No more sacrifices are offered in a temple in Jerusalem; His sacrifice on the cross was the final, perfect, sacrifice. Believers gathered in His Name are the temples of the living God – not just on Mount Zion, but in millions of places around the globe. The Body of Jesus Christ is about the Father's work in every nation: preaching and demonstrating the Kingdom, healing, and being perfected in holiness. And we have just seen that this plan extends beyond planet earth, to the infinity of the heavenly realms!

It all started with the call of one man: Abraham. Through the centuries God further revealed His plan, culminating in the life and teaching of His Son. There is a single flow of God's work – and it is moving toward the full manifestation of God's

Kingdom, with Jesus as King. The church is at the center of God's plan. It should be central in our lives as well.

8   REACHING THE SUMMIT

EPHESIANS 3:14–21

We have arrived at the end of chapter 3, and the end of the doctrinal foundation for the four steps we will study in chapters 4 through 6. Understanding these first chapters is essential to make it through those four steps successfully. Here we reach the summit of this letter, the heart of the Christian life, and one of the richest passages in the Bible.

It can take years of hard work to go through the steps of chapters 4-6, but what we see here is God's sovereign work. Without this experience of God's power and love, it will be impossible to make it through the four steps. That is why, before he starts them, Paul gets down on his knees. He knows he is on holy ground. He knows a supernatural work is needed to grasp the revelation he has written about. God's purposes, as Paul wrote about them in the first three chapters, form the basis of his prayer. When you pray for your family, church, or community, first seek God for his purpose in the situation, and then intercede for them based on that purpose.

In these verses - almost like Moses in Sinai - we will climb a mountain to a place of intimate communion with God. Let us approach the throne of God with reverence and humility, with hearts open to receive this great revelation.

Our Father...

¹⁴ For this reason I bow my knees before the Father, ¹⁵ from whom every family in heaven and on earth derives its name. (NASB)

What is your name? Who you are? In the Bible, a name is very important: It communicates the nature and essence of the person. When you came into this world, you were given your father's name. When you marry, your wife takes your name. Adam had the privilege of naming the animals, and you have the privilege of naming your children. Paul says that now you have a new name; you are born again into a new family: As an adopted son, you receive your Father's name, with all its privileges.

At first, the language seems a little confusing: What families is Paul talking about? Does he mean that even unbelieving families take their name from God? And what families are there in heaven? The context clarifies the confusion: Paul just finished talking about Jews and Gentiles being united in one family. He is speaking about the church, the family of believers - Jews and Gentiles - here on earth; and the church triumphant in heaven, those who have died in Christ. In fact, the best translation of the Greek *pasa patria* (every family) inserts "the:" *the entire family of God*. Your membership in his family provides two keys to experiencing all God has planned for you:

- The importance of relationship, family, and connecting with your Father and your brothers. The intimacy of home.
- Inclusion in a universal church from every age and nation. This is an immense vision: You are part of something very big.

The first request

[16] *that He would grant you, according to the riches of His glory, to be strengthened with power through His Spirit in the inner man.* (NASB)

Base Camp: Strengthened in the inner man

To climb a mountain you have to get in shape, through exercise and proper nutrition. That is true spiritually as well. If your inner man is weak, you will not be able to understand or experience what Paul is about to present.

- By what measure are you strengthened? *According to the riches of His glory*, which are impossible to measure. His resources are glorious and infinite. His strength and power is unlimited.
- With what are you strengthened? Power. You need power more than knowledge or anything material.
- Where? In the inner man. Many men who lift impressive weights every day in the gym are weak in the inner man. The only way to endure the trials, temptations, and battles of the four steps is with a strong inner man. Are you ready for them?
- How? By his Spirit. That means you want to do everything possible to facilitate the flow and fullness of the Spirit in your life. You can, and should, strengthen yourself by the means of grace (the Bible, prayer, fasting, the Lord's Supper, baptism, and participation in church), but here Paul is asking God to *grant* you this strength. A gift given, as the Spirit floods your life.

Have you experienced that power? Would you like to? What is the condition of your inner man? The ascent to intimate fellowship with God starts with a strong inner man. Weaklings will not make it.

Second request

17 so that Christ may dwell in your hearts through faith (NASB)

Then Christ will make his home in your hearts as you trust in him. (NLT)

Starting the climb: Christ dwelling in your heart

God strengthens us. That prepares our hearts for Christ to dwell there. Whether you feel it or not, you have experienced God's power, and by faith you believe that Christ dwells in you. Climbing the mountain, strengthened in the inner man, you *believe* you can reach the top.

At the beginning of the climb, in the cool of the morning, you realize you are not alone. You are part of a great company of brothers with the same destination. That in itself is exciting. Unfortunately, there are many on the climb who are so excited about that fellowship and the whole experience that they never realize God Himself dwells in their hearts. They do not have the faith to rely on someone they cannot see. They may spend a lifetime in church activities (like a sanctified social club) without a relationship to the living Christ. That is why Paul is compelled to pray this. We often assume that Christ dwells in the heart of every believer, but Paul knows that is not so.

Would you say you are experiencing the fullness of Christ dwelling in your heart? When He dwells there, He will fill you with his love, and you can go on to the next level.

Third request

17and that you, being rooted and grounded in love, (NASB)

Your roots will grow down into God's love and keep you strong. (NLT)

Strength in the heat of the day: Rooted and grounded in love

You have spent several hours (or months, or years) climbing. The cool of the morning has given way to a strong, burning sun. Your strength is fading. You are tired - and questioning the wisdom of trying such an intensive climb. Paul knows that without deep roots in God's love you will not have the strength to go on. Without those roots, many give up; they decide it is not worth it, and go back to base camp. They engage in church activities; even read their Bibles, pray, and listen to Christian music. But they never know the love of God.

Paul uses the Greek word *agape* for love, the unconditional love of God. God pours that love into your heart when you accept Jesus, and you experience it in communion with other brothers. To be rooted and grounded in love is to have a lifestyle of love.

Do you have those roots? Without love, you are nothing. Love is most important; like the deep roots of a tree that give it stability and nourishment, or the solid foundation that enables a house to withstand adversity and storms.

Many are content right here, drawing on God's love with these roots. For someone who has never known true love, it is a great blessing. At this point in the ascent, there are still green pastures, beautiful trees, and pleasant streams. You can already see that further up it gets windy and cold. You pass the tree line and the path is full of rocks. Many choose to stay where it is comfortable, believing that this is the blessed, prosperous, life that Christ promised us. Paul knows that only a supernatural work will keep us going, so he continues praying.

Fourth request

18 may be able to comprehend with all the saints what is the breadth and length and height and depth, 19 and to know the love of Christ which surpasses knowledge (NASB)

be fully capable of comprehending with all the saints (God's people) the width and length and height and depth of His love [fully experiencing that amazing, endless love]; and [that you may come] to know [practically, through personal experience] the love of Christ which far surpasses [mere] knowledge [without experience] (AMP)

Almost there: Knowing Christ's love

Now comes the full comprehension and experience of God's love. Although Paul speaks of the width, length, height, and depth of this love, obviously you cannot measure it. God sovereignly illumines your minds. His love is wide enough to include everyone. Its length is endless, for all of life and all eternity. It is deep enough to reach the worst sinner, and the depths of our discouragement and despair - even death. And its height lifts Christ to heaven and fills our hearts with worship.

It is only in the rich fellowship of brothers and sisters that we can fully understand this love. It is very difficult to experience love when you are alone!

Paul says God's love passes knowledge! We have to *experience* and *know* the love of Christ. It is not just something mental or intellectual. In this life, it is never possible to fully experience it, there is always more! It reminds me of what should happen in a marriage: As the years pass, and your knowledge of each other deepens, your love should grow. Would you say you are experiencing more and more of Christ's love? Or, after an initial flood when you first accepted Him, has your experience of His love dried up?

Last request

¹⁹that you may be filled to the measure of all the fullness of God.

Then you will be made complete with all the fullness of life and power that comes from God. (NLT)

that you may be filled up [throughout your being] to all the fullness of God [so that you may have the richest experience of God's presence in your lives, completely filled and flooded with God Himself]. (AMP)

The summit of the Christian life: Filled with all the fullness of God

It is possible to be filled with all the fullness of God! Are you full? Do you know anyone full of His fullness? You can have great knowledge of the Bible and theology, but if you do not know Christ's love, it will be impossible to be filled with His fullness. It flows from His love.

The Holy Spirit fills you with God's life and power. It begins with the baptism in the Spirit, but then you have to maintain the fullness of the Spirit with prayer, praise, and ministering to others with manifestations of his gifts. There is always more to experience! God is infinite!

Praise God!

²⁰ Now to him who is able to do immeasurably more than all we ask or imagine, according to his power that is at work within us, ²¹ to him be glory in the church and in Christ Jesus throughout all generations, for ever and ever! Amen.

Now to Him who is able to [carry out His purpose and] do superabundantly more than all that we dare ask or think [infinitely beyond our greatest prayers, hopes, or dreams], according to His power that is at work within us, to Him be the glory in the church and in Christ Jesus throughout all generations forever and ever. Amen. (AMP)

We have reached the summit. We are almost in heaven. We have to praise God! This doxology concludes this first half of Ephesians.

Now God is free to act in your life. He wants to - for His glory. He will amaze you with the amazing things He does for you, far beyond the prosperity promoted on television and in many churches. Way beyond requests for a new car or home or wealth. God can do exceeding more abundantly than all that we ask or imagine. You cannot even imagine the great things that God can do! Pray boldly, with great courage and faith.

You would like to stay here on the mountaintop with God. Indeed, you need to keep this perspective and maintain a strong inner man, rooted in God's love and filled with His Spirit. However, unfortunately, you are still here on this earth; you still have a job, family, temptations, and a battle with the devil. You have to go down and start the hard work of the four steps to mature manhood, but keep this intimacy with God!

The first part of Ephesians is full of theory and theology: the inclusion of Gentiles into God's people, the grace of God in our salvation, all things united in Christ, and the Church testifying to the rulers and powers of God's great wisdom. All that is very impressive, but it may not seem to have much to do with everyday life. You are about to enter four very practical steps that impact your life right now, but first you must deal with this matter of God's fullness and love.

The sad fact is that few people really know this kind of love. They have not gone up this mountain. They are not filled with all God's fullness. Sure, they may occasionally feel something like love in their hearts, but to be bathed in the love of Christ? Their lives motivated by his love? Few have that experience. If you have, you are very blessed. If it is not your experience, join with me in praying this prayer every day. We know it is God's will because it is in the Bible. Enough with spiritual poverty. Enough with all the material prosperity. It is time for spiritual prosperity. It is time to know this great love of God and be filled with His fullness. It is time to start the four steps and become a mature man. Are you ready?

THE FIRST STEP:

BE PART OF A HEALTHY CHURCH

9   GOD'S PLAN FOR THE CHURCH

EPHESIANS 4:1–3

The Ephesian church had an impressive beginning. It may have been Paul's most successful church plant. God blessed him with an anointed ministry and many manifestations of the Holy Spirit. Paul had provided them with a solid foundation, but he knew there was more. The longing of his heart was for them to reach maturity, so he wrote letters to instruct and encourage them. As with most of his letters, the first half deals with doctrine: who Christ is, what God has done for us, and who we are in Christ. But one thing stands out in those first three chapters: the emphasis on the church as the Body of Christ. Paul holds an extremely high view of the church and its place in God's plan. Not surprisingly, the first of the four essential steps to maturity is being part of a church that functions according to God's plan.

The Body of Christ in the first three chapters of Ephesians

To give us perspective, let's review what Paul has already said about the church:

God has put all things under the authority of Christ and has made him head over all things for the benefit of the church. (1:22, NLT)

Jesus has absolute and supreme authority as the undisputed head of the entire universe. In God's plan, that authority is primarily for the benefit of the church.

Which is His body, the fullness of Him Who fills all in all [for in that body lives the full measure of Him Who makes everything complete, and Who fills everything everywhere with Himself]. (1:23, AMP)

Here it explicitly states: the church *is* the Body of Christ. That is where He most fully dwells, and, more than anything else, it demonstrates who He is.

He made peace between Jews and Gentiles by creating in himself one new people from the two groups. Together as one body, Christ reconciled both groups to God by means of his death on the cross, and our hostility toward each other was put to death. (2:15-16, NLT)

Since creation, God has longed for His own people. A division had existed between His chosen people (the Jews), and the pagans (Gentiles), but Jesus died to bring peace and reconcile the two groups into one people. Any hostility or division between parts of Christ's body deeply grieve God.

Consequently, you are no longer foreigners and strangers, but fellow citizens with God's people and also members of his household, built on the foundation of the apostles and prophets, with Christ Jesus himself as the chief cornerstone. In him the whole building is joined together and rises to become a holy temple in the Lord. And in him you too are being built together to become a dwelling in which God lives by his Spirit. (2:19-22)

Paul has used the metaphor of the body to describe the church; now he introduces another metaphor: a house, or temple. God does not dwell in a building, but in His body: the people that form a local expression of his body, which is His family. Christ is the chief cornerstone and head of that temple, and the foundation is the ministry of the apostles and prophets. This is a holy temple, where God dwells by his Spirit. The church is pre-eminent in God's plan.

And this is God's plan: Both Gentiles and Jews who believe the Good News share equally in the riches inherited by God's children. Both are part of the same body, and both enjoy the promise of blessings because they belong to Christ Jesus. (3:6, NLT)

Everyone in the body of Christ (whether Jew or Gentile) enjoys all of God's riches and blessings.

God's purpose in all this was to use the church to display his wisdom in its rich variety to all the unseen rulers and authorities in the heavenly places. This was his eternal plan, which he carried out through Christ Jesus our Lord. (3:10-11, NLT)

God's eternal plan and purpose is to display who he is to the principalities and powers. How? Through the church! What testimony is the church giving in the heavenly realms? Don't you think God would do whatever it takes to make sure the church is giving a good testimony?

To him be glory in the church and in Christ Jesus throughout all generations, for ever and ever! Amen. (3:21)

We know that Christ glorified the Father, and continues to glorify Him, but the church is also supposed to glorify God. How is it doing? If not so well, that presents a huge problem. Any failure probably comes from not following God's plan for the church, which Paul so eloquently described in these first three chapters. If the church is that important, it is safe to say that it is impossible to reach maturity without involvement in a healthy church.

Your calling

4:1As a prisoner for the Lord, then, I urge you to live a life worthy of the calling you have received.

If you reflect on all the implications of these first three chapters, and the riches of God's call to repentance and new life, you cannot help but be amazed at all God has done for us. Paul gives us just one requirement at this point: walk worthy of that calling. A very high calling carries greater responsibility to conduct yourself accordingly.

We all have a general call to salvation, but every believer also has a specific call to a place of service in the Kingdom. Who are you? What role does God have for you? It may not be what you are doing right now. Paul wrote this letter as a prisoner. Some might say, "I guess my ministry is over. I can't do anything here in jail," but Paul knew God had called him to be an apostle. That calling does not change, no matter what the situation. As a prisoner, Paul continued ministering through letters and visits.

You may be trained as a carpenter, engineer, or businessman. That's great. In the world, those may be well-paying, important jobs, but God has His own calling or vocation for you. Jesus said,

"If you want to be great in his kingdom, you must become like a child." (Matthew 18:3) You may continue working in your career – but make sure that Christ is Lord of your job, or it can become an idol, especially if it takes priority over God's vocation for you. He calls you and assigns you a part in His kingdom. Whatever that calling is – even the most humble job – is very important to the Lord. If His Body is to function properly, you must do your part.

Yes, you are important in God's Kingdom! He needs you! The church needs you! At home and on the job, walk with your head held high, as the King's son. Walk worthy of your calling. It is not your choice. God calls you. He knows you, and exactly which job fits you perfectly. You can accept or reject that call, or struggle with it, as Moses did at the burning bush. I have known many men who run from it in their search for fame and fortune, and pay dearly for it.

Discovering your calling

Do you know what your calling is? Wait on the Lord, seek Him, and listen for His voice. God is going to use all your life experiences to prepare you for that calling.

How can you discover it?

- What stands out to you in the Bible? The miracles? Teaching? The prophets?

- What have you done that God has obviously blessed? How has He used you in the past?

- What have others said about you, especially those who know you best? For example, several family members may have commented that you would be a good pastor.

- Your pastor hopefully knows you well and has spiritual insight into your life. Ask Gim where he feels you should serve in the church.

- God may speak to you through a prophetic word, in prayer, or in the Scriptures

- What is the desire of your heart?

    ○ Do you long to see others healed? When you see someone sick, are you impressed to pray for them?

    ○ Do you love the Scriptures and find that other people understand them when you teach?

    ○ Do you have a burning desire to see others saved?

How to walk worthy of your calling

It should be obvious that to do God's work you should walk in such a way that He is glorified. Verses 2-3 contain four very important principles on how to walk worthy of your calling:

[2]Living as becomes you] with complete lowliness of mind (humility) and meekness (unselfishness, gentleness, mildness), with patience, bearing with one another and making allowances because you love one another. [3] Make every effort to keep the unity of the Spirit through the bond of peace. (AMP)

With complete humility. Generous, gentle, and humble service should characterize your ministry in the church. Pride is the source of many problems in the church; humility fosters harmony and unity.

With complete meekness. What man wants to be known as meek? We want to be bold and brave! But meekness is not weakness; it is the gentleness of someone who knows their strength and has control over it.

Bearing with one another. In patience, and unconditional, agape, love. Be tolerant, and quick to forgive others their faults. Make the same allowances for them that you would want them to make for you.

Do everything possible to keep the unity of the Spirit. Unity cannot be created - we already have it because we share the same Spirit. It is our responsibility to protect and keep that unity, always on the lookout for anything that could cause division, and eager to be a peacemaker. Divisions within and between churches are a stumbling block for the world, which says, "They talk about love, but are always fighting!"

You may have spent years preparing for your career, and may be very successful. That's great, but we are talking here about the God of the universe calling you to serve in His Son's body. We have seen how important the church is in His plan for eternity. To take your place in the church and begin moving to mature manhood, you must find out what God is calling you to do in that body, and walk worthy of it.

10 A HEALTHY CHURCH

EPHESIANS 4:4–16

So far in Ephesians we have seen the pre-eminence of the church in God's plan. The church *is* the Body of Christ. It is a concept that Paul further develops in 1 Corinthians 12: diversity within the unity of that body. We are all different, with distinct gifts, callings, and personalities. That's good. Unity does not mean uniformity, but we must start with a clear understanding of all we share in common. Since we are so diverse, we must focus on the unity we already have, and do everything possible to maintain it.

Our Unity

Seven times in these verses, Paul uses the word "one":

⁴ For there is one body and one Spirit, just as you have been called to one glorious hope for the future. ⁵ There is one Lord, one faith, one baptism, ⁶ and one God and Father, who is over all and in all and living through all.

1. Christ only has *one body*. No matter what denomination or group you may belong to, every true believer is part of that universal church. When Jesus returns there will be just one wedding, and one bride waiting for Him.
2. There is *one Spirit*, which dwells within every believer.

91

3. There is only *one Lord and Savior*, Jesus Christ, who is the head of every local expression of His body (each local church).

4. There is *one God and Father*. He is God over all, in all, and through all. Our Father has only one family. For anyone who says the trinity is not biblical, notice how clearly these three persons are defined in these verses.

5. There is *one baptism*, even though it is administered in a variety of ways.

6. We all share in *one and the same hope*: Eternal life in His kingdom.

7. There is only *one saving faith*: in Jesus and what He did on the cross, and in God's Word.

Do you have this concept of unity when you meet brothers and sisters from other churches? We are called to pursue peace and reconciliation, and work together with them. We are not in competition – just as there is no competition between your hand and your foot. Both have a crucial part to play, and they need to work together, each doing their work, and not competing with each other. Someone might say that they want to work for the Lord, but do not want to work with anyone else. God's work is based on love, and the importance of each member of the body. It is impossible to fully experience the Christian life by yourself. It is not easy, but we are to patiently bear with others and their faults.

Diversity in the unity

In the midst of that unity there is a very important "but:" God is one, *but* we are many, with many different callings.

⁷ But he has given each one of us a special gift through the generosity of Christ. (NLT)

Being different is good. Some prefer a quiet worship service, others want to shout and dance. Both are fine and can be in God's will. There is room for great variety within the body of Christ.

The Greek word (*charism*), translated "gift" here, can also be translated "grace." Every believer has at least one spiritual gift – given as God determines would be best for you. You don't deserve it, and you can't earn it. It is not given to you because you are such a good Christian or so mature, but because Jesus loves to give generously.

⁸ That is why the Scriptures say,

"When he ascended to the heights,
*   he led a crowd of captives*
*   and gave gifts to his people."*

⁹ Notice that it says "he ascended." This clearly means that Christ also descended to our lowly world. ¹⁰ And the same one who descended is the one who ascended higher than all the heavens, so that he might fill the entire universe with himself.

Paul cites Psalm 68 as prophesying the gifts that would be given believers when Christ ascended, starting at Pentecost. Jesus humbled himself and lived among us – and was exalted by His Father. As Philippians 2 says, Christ was lifted up to the highest place, at the Father's right hand, governing and filling the whole universe. To go up, first you have to come down. God wants to lift you up, but first you have to humble yourself, following our Lord's example.

Five offices in the church

[11] So Christ himself gave the apostles, the prophets, the evangelists, the pastors, and teachers.

Among these gifts are five offices Christ endued with His authority, which establish and lead His church. There is order among them, with apostles first:

Apostle means "sent;" by the Lord (and usually another church), to establish and supervise local churches. They are responsible for maintaining sound doctrine and the purity of the church, and have special spiritual authority.

Prophets. Anyone can have the *spiritual gift* of prophecy (see 1 Corinthians 14), which is for encouragement and comfort. The person in the *office* of prophet usually travels among churches, often with a message of correction or guidance, or with insight into future events.

Evangelists. Everyone should evangelize, but the evangelist has a special anointing. Their message may not be much different, but God has called them and will use them to reach many with the Gospel.

Pastors care for and feed God's flock. There is a great need today for pastors with a true heart of love for their sheep. Some who are pastoring churches actually are evangelists or teachers. Others are like the hired hand of John 10:12 – pursuing their own agenda and ignoring the real needs of their flock.

Teachers have special ability to make God's Word clear. The church is in need of instruction.

The purpose of these offices

[12] *Their responsibility is to equip God's people to do his work and build up the church, the body of Christ.* (NLT)

To establish a church, each of these offices must be functioning. They don't do all the work, but rather equip God's people so *they* can do the work. Each member of the church ministers according to their calling and gifting. Some pastors, out of ignorance or insecurity, do not want others ministering in their church. They feel they have to do everything – and often get burned out in the process. A church dominated by a pastor who does not let the gifts function can only grow to the limit of that pastor's abilities – and will suffer when that pastor leaves.

The goal

[13] *[That it might develop] until we all attain oneness in the faith and in the comprehension of the [full and accurate] knowledge of the Son of God, that [we might arrive] at really mature manhood (the completeness of personality which is nothing less than the standard height of Christ's own perfection), the measure of the stature of the fullness of the Christ and the completeness found in Him.* (AMP)

What are we aiming for in the church's ministry?

- Attaining true unity among all believers, embracing the same faith and teaching of the Gospel.

- Attaining full and accurate knowledge of Jesus that results in intimate fellowship with him.

- Reaching maturity as men and women of God.

- Experiencing the fullness and completeness of Christ in our daily lives.

Wow! That is a high calling! How many people do you know who have achieved that? Is it possible we haven't because these offices and gifts are not functioning according to God's plan?

The actual condition of many believers

[14] Then we will no longer be immature like children. We won't be tossed and blown about by every wind of new teaching. We will not be influenced when people try to trick us with lies so clever they sound like the truth. (NLT)

[14] So then, we may no longer be children, tossed [like ships] to and fro between chance gusts of teaching and wavering with every changing wind of doctrine, [the prey of] the cunning and cleverness of unscrupulous men, [engaged] in every shifting form of trickery in inventing errors to mislead. (AMP)

Unfortunately, I find this verse describes many Christians:

- They are like unstable children.

- They grab onto every new teaching that comes along.

  o One day they hear some prophet on TV and get excited about his word.

- o The next day a new apostle comes to town with another teaching.

- o The result is great confusion. That is why God places us in a local church with a pastor whose word we can trust. I would not say it is wrong to listen to anyone on TV or the internet, but be very careful!

- Believe it or not, there are many unscrupulous people out there, deceivers, who are like wolves in sheep's clothing. Jesus warned they would multiply in the last days!

  - o The church is full of people pursuing their own agendas and establishing their own kingdoms. They constantly ask for money and are very good at deceiving people.

  - o They invent errors that mislead God's people, or are inspired by the devil to invent them. The person not firmly grounded in the Word is easily led astray.

How can you tell when a church is functioning properly?

- There will be stability.

- Instead of children who are up and down all the time, there will be men unshakable in their faith.

- There will be solid knowledge of the Bible and its teachings.

God's will for your church

15 *Instead, we will speak the truth in love, growing in every way more and more like Christ, who is the head of his body, the church.* 16 *He makes the whole body fit together perfectly. As each part does its own special work, it helps the other parts grow, so that the whole body is healthy and growing and full of love.* (NLT)

15 *Rather, let our lives lovingly express truth [in all things, speaking truly, dealing truly, living truly]. Enfolded in love, let us grow up in every way and in all things into Him Who is the Head, [even] Christ (the Messiah, the Anointed One).* 16 *For because of Him the whole body (the church, in all its various parts), closely joined and firmly knit together by the joints and ligaments with which it is supplied, when each part [with power adapted to its need] is working properly [in all its functions], grows to full maturity, building itself up in love.* (AMP)

- Follow the truth – in love. Speak it and live it. A mature man needs both truth and love: Love without truth is weak and wishy washy; truth without love is harsh. The combination is powerful.

- Become increasingly like Christ. Others should see Christ's presence in your church and your life. Growth is an integral part of being a Christian. If you are not growing, there is probably something wrong.

- Christ's body should be functioning smoothly, with Him as the head, and every part in its place, doing its job, helping each other and growing together in love.

Does that sound like your church? Are you even in a church? If so, is it healthy? Does it reflect this picture of the church as God designed it? Are you operating in your calling? Is some adjustment needed in your church?

This is the very foundation of growth to maturity. If your church experience is deficient, you will find the next steps practically impossible to achieve. I have observed many Christians working very hard at the next three steps who are constantly frustrated, because they have never laid the foundation of this critical step. In over forty years as a believer, I have been in countless churches, but rarely have I seen a church that truly is following this simple plan. It is not complicated – but it is not easy, either. Perhaps because Satan knows it is so powerful, he has worked in every way possible to keep the church from fulfilling its destiny.

SECOND STEP:

WALKING IN HOLINESS AND THE POWER OF THE HOLY SPIRIT

11 ARE YOU SAVED?

EPHESIANS 4:17–19, 22; 5:5–6

Warning!

It is very dangerous to start on this path to maturity alone! You will encounter many difficulties that are almost impossible to overcome without the support of Christian brothers. You will also encounter many hypocrites and others who call themselves Christians, but are living for their own pleasure. God intends for the church, established according to the plan we have studied in Ephesians 4, to be the foundation for the rest of the Christian life. Of course there is no perfect church, but ask the Lord for a church that:

- Preaches and teaches the Bible, and sincerely tries to put it into practice.
- Lifts up and glorifies the Lord in their worship.
- Has a pastor who truly loves his people.
- Allows the Holy Spirit freedom to move.
- Demonstrates Christ-like love among the brothers and sisters.
- Maintains a good testimony as salt and light in the community, where they serve and share the good news.

There is a second, even more serious, danger as you begin this journey: You must know Jesus. That may sound obvious, but the church is full of unsaved people:

- They go to services and activities.
- They carry Bibles and may know what it says.
- They sing and may even dance in the services.

But...

- A completely different person comes out at night when they are on the computer.
- Or at school, where they cheat and have filthy mouths.
- Or at work, where they steal time and office supplies from their employer.
- Or at home, where they are abusive to their wives and kids.
- Or with their buddies, drinking and sharing dirty jokes.

It is not easy being a Christian, but there is no excuse for sin. Before taking the next step to maturity, something very important must be resolved: The issue of your salvation. It is very easy to be deceived here.

Are you saved?

[17] *So I tell you this, and insist on it in the Lord, that you must no longer live as the Gentiles do, in the futility of their thinking.*

...in their perverseness [in the folly, vanity, and emptiness of their souls and the futility] of their minds. (AMP)

With the Lord's authority I say this: Live no longer as the Gentiles do, for they are hopelessly confused. (NLT)

The question here is, "How are you living?" Since you are reading this, we probably share similar beliefs:

- Jesus is the Son of God who came to this world, died on the cross, and rose from the dead.
- We are saved through faith in Jesus, given a new life, and forgiven for our sin.
- We will spend eternity in heaven.
- The Bible is God's Word, true and authoritative.

That is important, but James says demons also believe that – and tremble (James 2:19). To be saved, those beliefs need to influence your daily life. In Matthew 7:21-23 Jesus said:

> *"Not everyone who says to me, 'Lord, Lord,' will enter the kingdom of heaven, but only the one who does the will of my Father who is in heaven. Many will say to me on that day, 'Lord, Lord, did we not prophesy in your name and in your name drive out demons and in your name perform many miracles?' Then I will tell them plainly, 'I never knew you. Away from me, you evildoers!'*

Your faith must affect how you live. Paul *insists* on it, with the Lord's authority. It is not an option for the super-spiritual. If you are saved, you cannot live like people in the world. There are only two roads, two options:

- The wide road that leads to death, where we all start.
- The narrow road, walking with Jesus.

How does the world live?

Most of us already know only too well how the world lives. Verse 17 is the first step on a downward spiral that ends in death – similar to what Paul describes in the first chapters of Romans. These steps probably describe what your life was like in the past – and the lives of most of the people you know. The various translations help us understand more clearly what God wants to say to us here. It all starts in the mind:

1. Their thinking is futile, empty, and perverse. They are hopelessly confused. The world has a warped sense of wisdom and of what is important. Watch a show on TV or read some Facebook posts: Their thinking is distorted and corrupt; they aren't thinking clearly.

[18] *They are darkened in their understanding and separated from the life of God because of the ignorance that is in them due to the hardening of their hearts.*

Their minds are full of darkness; they wander far from the life God gives because they have closed their minds and hardened their hearts against him. (NLT)

They've refused for so long to deal with God that they've lost touch not only with God but with reality itself. They can't think straight anymore. (MSG)

2. Their understanding is darkened, so they cannot understand spiritual truth. It is not surprising that they do not accept the Gospel – it seems foolish when you are far from God and relying on your own thinking. Many today want a designer Christianity, picking and choosing what they like about Jesus and following Him their own way, but never submitting to Him as Lord.

3. With their minds darkened, they wander hopelessly lost in a fog. They need light: The light of the Word, and the light of God. There is also another light: We are the light of the world! Live in such a way that your light shines in the darkness.

4. They are separated from the life of God – spiritually and eternally dead.

5. They are ignorant. They lack biblical knowledge. They know about Jesus, but have never truly heard the Gospel. That is not necessarily their fault – how can they believe if no one shares the Word of God with them?

6. They have hardened their hearts to God. There is no spiritual interest, or desire to change. Only the Holy Spirit can penetrate a hardened heart. Be careful you don't harden your own heart!

[19] *Having lost all sensitivity, they have given themselves over to sensuality so as to indulge in every kind of impurity, and they are full of greed.*

They have no sense of shame. They live for lustful pleasure and eagerly practice every kind of impurity. (NLT)

In their spiritual apathy they have become callous and past feeling and reckless and have abandoned themselves to unbridled sensuality, eager and greedy to indulge in every form of impurity [that their depraved desires may suggest and demand]. (AMP)

7. Any sense of shame or sensitivity to the perversity they are living in has been lost. As they give themselves over to sensuality and live in sin, their conscience is seared.

8. They abandon themselves to live for lustful pleasure, which has become their god. It is a conscious decision, the result of perverse thinking. And if you don't know God, why not? Let's eat, drink, and be merry, for tomorrow we die.

9. Eagerly and greedily, they indulge in every kind of impurity. They cannot get enough – they are never satisfied, but pursue ever greater perversity. All inhibition is gone – and they want you to take part in their sin: *They are surprised that you do not join them in their reckless, wild living, and they heap abuse on you.* (1 Peter 4:4)

The old nature is [22]*being corrupted by its deceitful desires* (NIV), *by lust and deception.* (NLT)

10. Without Christ, your lust corrupts you, leaving you completely deceived. What looks so attractive never truly satisfies.

Reflect on these steps

Do they describe your past life? Or, if you are honest, do they describe you now? We were all hopelessly lost. The Christian is no better than these people in the world, but you will be subject to a more severe judgment if you live like that after accepting Christ. If this describes you, something is very wrong. You have probably been deceived. You may have gone forward in a service, prayed a prayer, and been told that you are saved and going to heaven. But listen to what God's Word says in Ephesians 5:5-6:

For of this you can be sure: No immoral, impure or greedy person—such a person is an idolater—has any inheritance in the kingdom of Christ and of God.[6] Let no one deceive you with empty words, for because of such things God's wrath comes on those who are disobedient.

You can be sure that no immoral, impure, or greedy person will inherit the Kingdom of Christ and of God. For a greedy person is an idolater, worshiping the things of this world. Don't be fooled by those who try to excuse these sins, for the anger of God will fall on all who disobey him. (NLT)

Don't be deceived – you cannot go on living like that and be saved. Of course, no one is perfect; we all sin, but the true Christian is convicted of his sin and goes running to his Savior, repentant, and asking forgiveness. Paul is speaking here of the person who continues to practice and live in these sins. Unfortunately, there are many greedy people in the church, who worship the things of this world. Even worse, many preachers actually encourage that idolatry. It is not possible to walk both roads, even though many people want to.

Many false teachers today deceive people with a message they want to hear: you can live as you want; sin is not that serious. However, the Word of God says those very things are bringing God's wrath on us. There is judgment coming – and there may be some surprises. Don't be deceived by those who try to justify sin. They are the sons of disobedience, not the sons of God, and they are the ones who will experience God's wrath.

Many people in the world think they are going to heaven, but are sadly deceived. God wants to save you from that deception. There is a healthy fear of God – fear of hell and eternal punishment. Christ died to set you free from that sin. There is hope for you. God has something much better for you, something you have already gotten a taste of in Ephesians. When I was a prison chaplain I met many pastors who had been ministering in churches for years – and realized they were never saved. They accepted Christ in prison and were gloriously transformed by His power. It is possible that the Lord is speaking to you right now, opening your eyes to realize you're not saved: You are still on that wide road, living just like everyone else in the world. You are trying to serve two masters – but Jesus said that is impossible. Go back to the beginning of Ephesians and read the first three chapters. Accept what God has done for you, repent of your sin, and give your life to Jesus, to follow Him on that narrow road.

12 REPENTANCE

EPHESIANS 4:20–24

Do you know Jesus as your Lord and Savior? Are you part of a church seeking to follow God's plan, as Paul describes it in Ephesians 4:16? *He makes the whole body fit together perfectly. As each part does its own special work, it helps the other parts grow, so that the whole body is healthy and growing and full of love.*

If your answer is "yes," you are ready for the next step to maturity.

A daily life that reflects and glorifies Jesus Christ

This is a big step, which takes up considerable space in Paul's letter. It is common today, as it was then, to excuse sin and rationalize a worldly lifestyle. Paul is certain they know better; he had invested himself in them for an entire year. Imagine anointed teaching every day about the cost of discipleship, Jesus' Lordship, and the need for holiness! He could say with confidence:

4:20 But you did not learn Christ in this way, 21 if indeed you have heard Him and have been taught in Him, just as truth is in Jesus. (NASB)

What have you learned about Christ? Unfortunately, there is a lot of unbiblical teaching out there. We have to carefully examine every teaching in the light of the Word. It is hard, but you may find it necessary to reject some things a beloved pastor has taught.

Paul is also aware that some receive sound instruction from the best teachers and still do not grow. Why?

- They did not hear. Remember how often Jesus said, "*He who has ears to hear let him hear*"? God has to open your understanding to hear the truth. If you are not saved, or have a hard heart, you probably will not hear. Many people hear only what they want to hear, or maybe they are just thinking about their wives or plans for the rest of the day, or are too busy playing with their smart phones.

- They were not taught in (or by) Christ, did not have the Holy Spirit to teach them how to walk, or were simply unteachable.

If you are a pastor who has taught the Bible, and your people still are not growing, this might explain it. But many simply lack the genuine repentance necessary to start on this second step to maturity.

Genuine repentance

[22] *You were taught, with regard to your former way of life, to put off your old self, which is being corrupted by its deceitful desires.*

Throw off your old sinful nature and your former way of life, which is corrupted by lust and deception. (NLT)

*Strip yourselves of your former nature [put off and discard your
old unrenewed self] which characterized your previous manner
of life and becomes corrupt through lusts and desires that spring
from delusion.* (AMP)

The old self, the sinful nature, is corrupted by lust and
deception. Take it off, like dirty clothes beyond saving,
repairing, or washing, and put on the new nature, like a new set
of clothes. You cannot grow with those old clothes on. Get rid
of them. As the NLT says of the old nature: *throw* it off.

This is what we call *repentance*. It sounds easy: just take off the
old clothes and put on the new. However, like a well-worn pair
of jeans (anyone else hate to give up favorite jeans?), those old
clothes can be very comfortable. You are used to them. They
are fashionable. You do not know what the new clothes will be
like, and you cannot even try them on them. You have to put
them on in faith that somehow God knows what is going to look
good on you. You can get an idea of what they are like by
looking at other people in their new clothes.

It is like Israel when they came out of slavery in Egypt: Life was
hard there, but they were used to it, and it actually seemed
preferable to the fear and uncertainty of a journey to an
unknown Promised Land. In repentance, you leave your
slavery, and start on a journey to a new life. God has something
much better for you than the ugly, dirty rags you were used to.

New clothes

Paul uses clothing to help us understand repentance. Another
symbol is water baptism: a radical identification with Christ in
His death, burial, and resurrection. The old man is dead –

crucified and nailed to the cross. It's not easy to crucify yourself, but God promises to gloriously resurrect you to a new life.

If you are still wearing the old clothes of your sinful nature, you can take them off and throw them away right now. And don't worry; God will not leave you naked. He has new clothes ready for you.

God's image restored

[24] *Put on the new self, created to be like God in true righteousness and holiness.*

And put on the new nature (the regenerate self) created in God's image, [Godlike] in true righteousness and holiness. (AMP)

Holiness is not about mind control, laws, or rules. It has nothing to do with your own efforts. It is about a God-given, totally new, nature. First, you have to decide to take the step, and get rid of your old nature. Sorry, but you cannot hold onto your old clothes, just in case you occasionally want to go casual (or sinful). Some get rid of the old man without putting on new clothes; others grab onto the flashy clothes of prosperity and happiness that the world and Satan offer. They are very deceptive. Go with what God has given – put on a whole new nature. You certainly do not want to be naked and unprotected. In Christ, everything is made new: You are a new man, born again, and created to be like God. Did you catch that? Do you see how the Amplified translates it? *Godlike!* No, you do not become God, but your new nature is created *in God's image.* Does that sound familiar? That is how God created Adam! In Christ, God's original intention for us is restored! God wants to bring us back to that relationship He had with Adam and Eve before their fall!

True righteousness and holiness

Your new nature is created in righteousness; Jesus' righteousness, received by faith. It is not your righteousness, because your righteousness is still like filthy rags. God declares you not guilty; free from the punishment you deserve for your rebellion. The new nature is also created in holiness: You are part of a new community set apart and different from the world.

God offers all of this to you, free of charge. You don't deserve it. You can't earn it or buy it. You just have to get to the end of yourself. Are you ready for a complete transformation? Are you tired of all your own efforts to change? If you have accepted Jesus, you already have that new nature; God has already given you new clothes. Now you have to learn how to wear them, how to walk in that God-like nature. Again, it is similar to Israel's experience leaving Egypt: They were already free, but it took forty years to learn how to walk with God. Many times they wanted to go back and put on the old clothes of their slavery. Burn those clothes! They cannot work for you anymore! If you try to go back and put them on again, you will find they do not fit. They are beyond repair.

Thank God for giving you His own nature and restoring His image in you! He has done His part – now it is up to you to accept it, believe it, and put on that new nature. Then the hard work begins.

Be made new!

²³ *You were taught, with regard to your former way of life, to be made new in the attitude of your minds.*

Let the Spirit renew your thoughts and attitudes. (NLT)

Be constantly renewed in the spirit of your mind [having a fresh mental and spiritual attitude]. (AMP)

The same teaching that calls us to put off the old man and put on the new nature, also commands us to be made new in our minds, thoughts, and attitudes. This verse serves as a bridge between the old man, whom we have thrown off, and the new man, created in God's image. You already have that God-like nature – but I doubt that you are anywhere near the mature man described in 4:13. The road to maturity starts with your life in the church, learning about real love as you deal with others in their weaknesses. Now a second process has to start inside you: You are responsible to renew your mind. That's hard work. That's discipleship.

We have all tried to change something in our lives, but unless your mind is changed, it will not happen. Transformation starts in your thoughts and attitudes. Once they are transformed, your daily life will be impacted.

Paul uses the word *spirit* here in talking about our inner world. The New Living Translation chooses to see that spirit as referring to the *Holy Spirit* – and our need to let *Him* renew our thoughts and attitudes. Although, technically, the more generic translation is probably correct, I think there is truth in both: We have to allow the Holy Spirit to work in us, but there are also conscious steps we must take to renew our minds. If you continue to fill it with the world's garbage, you cannot expect the Spirit to miraculously renew and cleanse it. The Spirit gives you the power to make wise decisions in how you fill your mind and how you think; He makes Scripture come alive to transform you.

What are your thoughts and attitudes like? Meditate on the Bible, on what is true. Fill your mind with praise to God. How is your old man doing? Still alive? Are you holding onto your old clothes? Get rid of them! Crucify the old man and nail your sin to Jesus' cross!

> *Since, then, you have been raised with Christ, set your hearts on things above, where Christ is, seated at the right hand of God. Set your minds on things above, not on earthly things. For you died, and your life is now hidden with Christ in God. When Christ, who is your life, appears, then you also will appear with him in glory. Put to death, therefore, whatever belongs to your earthly nature: sexual immorality, impurity, lust, evil desires and greed, which is idolatry.* (Colossians 3:1-5)

13 FIVE AREAS IMPACTED BY A GENUINE REPENTANCE

EPHESIANS 4:25 - 5:3

There is no way the old, sinful, man can somehow be rehabilitated and reach maturity. The only solution is to crucify him, take off those old clothes, and put on the new man, created in God's image. That is a gift from God, but there is a part for you to play in that transformation (4:23):

Be made new in the attitude of your minds.

Yes, my brother, you play an essential part in this process. Here we will look at five key areas that may need an attitude adjustment.

Your speech

[25] *Therefore each of you must put off falsehood and speak truthfully to your neighbor, for we are all members of one body.*

So stop telling lies. Let us tell our neighbors the truth, for we are all parts of the same body. (NLT)

Stop lying. Did you know lying is a problem for many Christians? Is it for you? Many actually live a lie, and are not even aware of it. A lie starts a vicious cycle: you have to cover yourself with another lie. Lying is serious. Satan is the father of lies. Revelation 21:8 says *All liars…will be consigned to the fiery lake of burning sulfur.*

The requirement is very simple: always tell the truth. Be transparent, with nothing to hide. In the church, we are all part of the same body. Lies destroy trust and fellowship, and create conflict.

29 *Do not let any unwholesome talk come out of your mouths, but only what is helpful for building others up according to their needs, that it may benefit those who listen.*

Don't use foul or abusive language. Let everything you say be good and helpful, so that your words will be an encouragement to those who hear them. (NLT)

Eliminate unwholesome talk. Think before you speak – and make sure whatever you say builds others up and encourages them. Think about their needs, and let your words benefit to them. Are you still talking like you used to on the street? Is your language different at work or at home than at church? Do you have a filthy mouth with your friends? Your words reveal what is in your heart.

I have noticed something common among Christians who carefully avoid foul language: a way of joking that puts down their brothers in Christ. They may laugh, but the subtle jabs often hurt, and are a direct violation of this command to always build others up. Many Christians also get into grumbling and complaining, or talking down the government, the church, or someone else. That can become a cancer in the church. Make sure whatever you say benefits and blesses the other person.

5:4 *Nor should there be obscenity, foolish talk or coarse joking, which are out of place, but rather thanksgiving.*

Get rid of all obscenity, foolish talk, and coarse joking. Be careful of who you hang out with. If you spend time with guys who tell dirty jokes and use obscenities, chances are you will too. If you fill your mind with that kind of talk on the internet or TV, it will probably enter your conversation. Foolish talk is trickier. I suspect we try to justify a lot of foolish talk. The tongue is powerful. God gave it to you to bless others and build them up, and to praise Him and give Him thanks.

> The tongue is a small part of the body, but it makes great boasts. Consider what a great forest is set on fire by a small spark. The tongue also is a fire, a world of evil among the parts of the body. It corrupts the whole body, sets the whole course of one's life on fire, and is itself set on fire by hell.
>
> All kinds of animals, birds, reptiles and sea creatures are being tamed and have been tamed by mankind, but no human being can tame the tongue. It is a restless evil, full of deadly poison.
>
> With the tongue we praise our Lord and Father, and with it we curse human beings, who have been made in God's likeness. Out of the same mouth come praise and cursing. My brothers and sisters, this should not be. Can both fresh water and salt water flow from the same spring? (James 3:5-11)

Your anger

4:26 Be angry, and yet do not sin; do not let the sun go down on your anger, 27 and do not give the devil an opportunity. (NASB)

And "don't sin by letting anger control you." Don't let the sun go down while you are still angry, for anger gives a foothold to the devil. (NLT)

"In your anger do not sin": Do not let the sun go down while you are still angry, and do not give the devil a foothold.

In the Greek, it is a command, as the New American Standard translates it: Be angry! What freedom! It is all right to be angry! It is not a sin! God gets angry! Ephesians 5:6 talks about God's wrath against our sin. We too should hate sin and get angry about it. Yet many Christians are afraid of anger because it has caused them so much trouble in the past. It is a very strong emotion that can easily lead to sin. Paul gives three commands:

- Do not sin in your anger. Control it, instead of letting it control you. It is fine to express your anger in a calm and controlled manner. It is not okay to hurt others or destroy something in your anger.
- Do not let the sun go down on your anger. Be slow to anger – and quick to forgive and resolve the situation. Do not hold a grudge or let a root of bitterness grow in your heart.
- Do not give the devil a foothold. When you are angry, it is easy to say things you will regret later, which can do great damage. Anger opens a door to the devil. Be alert to his deception, and ready to rebuke him and call out to Jesus when you are struggling with anger.

Anger is so problematic (and so misunderstood) that I am dedicating the next chapter to a study on what the Bible says about it.

Your work

28 Anyone who has been stealing must steal no longer, but must work, doing something useful with their own hands, that they may have something to share with those in need.

It is well known that Ten Commandments say, "Do not steal." However, there is a much deeper principle here than simply not robbing someone. The thief thinks only about himself; it does not matter how his theft may affect someone else, and he is definitely not thinking about helping those in need (unless he is Robin Hood!). Unfortunately, many Christians steal from their jobs; little things like time, pencils, or copies.

God is a hard worker *("My Father is always at his work to this very day, and I too am working."* Jesus, in John 5:17) Work is good. Do something useful with your hands, not so you can get rich and buy lots of things, but to generously share with those in need.

Do you help the needy? Are you working? I know that can be touchy in a time of high unemployment, when it is hard to find a good job. But don't turn to something illegal! Keep busy in something productive. There is truth in that old saying "an idle mind is the devil's workshop."

Your relationships

31 Get rid of all bitterness, rage, anger, harsh words, and slander, as well as all types of evil behavior. 32 Instead, be kind to each other, tenderhearted, forgiving one another, just as God through Christ has forgiven you. (NLT)

Let all bitterness and indignation and wrath (passion, rage, bad temper) and resentment (anger, animosity) and quarreling (brawling, clamor, contention) and slander (evil-speaking, abusive or blasphemous language) be banished from you, with all malice (spite, ill will, or baseness of any kind). And become useful and helpful and kind to one another, tenderhearted (compassionate, understanding, loving-hearted), forgiving one another [readily and freely], as God in Christ forgave you. (AMP)

Do you want to be a good friend and a good husband? Here are a few things to get rid of that damage relationships. The Amplified Bible is a mouthful to read, but it gives you the whole picture of what is involved here. In brief, take off:

- Bitterness
- Rage and anger
- Harsh words (You would be surprised at how many Christian men are guilty here!)
- Slander (any false or defamatory words spoken about a person)
- All types of evil behavior

In their place, make it a point to be:

- Kind to each other. It is amazing how much difference simple kindness can make in a home!
- Tenderhearted. Some people may call a tenderhearted man a softie, but that is what fosters good relationships.
- Forgiving.

We have a great example of how to forgive: Jesus. You are to forgive as God has forgiven you through Christ. That is a gift. You received grace and forgiveness from God, now he calls you to forgive others. (*For if you forgive other people when they sin against you, your heavenly Father will also forgive you. But if you do not forgive others their sins, your Father will not forgive your sins.* Matthew 6:14-15)

How is it going for you on this softer side? Is there something you need to get rid of that is damaging your relationships? Is your heart tender? Or has it become hardened, even toward your wife or children? Is there someone you need to forgive?

Your idols: Sex and money

5:3 But among you there must not be even a hint of sexual immorality, or of any kind of impurity, or of greed, because these are improper for God's holy people.

Wow. Sexual sin and greed. Those two things probably dominate most men's lives. Our culture prods us to lust and covet. The main battle in most men's minds is sex; it is so powerful that you can hardly mention it without falling into sin. You know how it is: You see a woman on the street or on TV and suddenly you're turned on. You cannot play around here. This is where many men lose the battle. The only solution is to recognize it for what it is, and be very vigilant. This is such a serious battle that chapter 15 will offer more help in maintaining sexual purity.

Suffice it to say here that if you are to grow in Christ, you have to get rid of sexual sin and greed. There should not be even a *hint* of them in your life. They should never even be *mentioned*.

The sad reality for most people is that not only is there a hint, they are *bombarded* with them on TV and in movies. Even worse, many men are addicted to internet porn.

Greed is defined as a selfish and excessive consumption or desire for more of something than is needed, such as food, wealth, or power. It can also be called covetousness. That is another of the Ten Commandments: Do not covet. Unfortunately, greed could describe most Americans – even the Christians. And we have exported our greed to the rest of the world, often dressing it with spiritual words. Advertising is everywhere, and friends and family constantly pressure you to buy more. Learn to be content with what God has given you!

The bottom line: Imitate God and live a life of love

5:1 *Imitate God, therefore, in everything you do, because you are his dear children.* 2 *Live a life filled with love, following the example of Christ. He loved us and offered himself as a sacrifice for us, a pleasing aroma to God.* (NLT)

Have you had a child who watched you and imitated your every move? Do the same with God! Study Him, watch Him, and imitate Him as a beloved son. You cannot imitate someone you do not know, so spend quality time with Him. We have a great model to follow here: Jesus Christ. A few years back everyone was asking, "What would Jesus do?" Live out the same love Christ has for us. He laid down His life for you. That ultimate sacrifice was a pleasing offering to His Father. Can you make the same offering? Make it your aim to love as Jesus does.

If you were to make this one simple decision – to love like Jesus and imitate your heavenly Father – your life would be transformed. Try it for a week and see what happens.

Is there evidence of a genuine repentance in your life? Are you walking in holiness? Do you truly desire sexual purity? Are you greedy? Here are five essential battlefields to conquer on the road to maturity. They trip up Christians today, just as they did 2000 years ago. In your own strength, you will never make it, but thank God, He has made a provision for you. When you have truly repented and determined to put off these sins, you are ready for the fullness of the Holy Spirit. The final part of this second passage to mature manhood is learning to walk in his power. But first, we will dedicate two chapters to two of the deepest struggles for many men: anger and sex.

14 BE ANGRY, BUT DO NOT SIN

We studied what Ephesians says about anger in the previous chapter, but I have known so many men who struggle with anger that I want to dedicate an entire chapter to it. If it is not a problem for you, move on to the next chapter, on sex, which is a struggle for almost every man.

What the Bible says about God's anger

Anger is not bad. Read the Old Testament! God is an angry god, with His fierce anger often burning against His people. That anger is very powerful, even destructive:

We are consumed by your anger and terrified by your indignation. If only we knew the power of your anger! Your wrath is as great as the fear that is your due. (Psalm 90:7, 11)

That was written by Moses, a man who certainly had seen God's wrath, but also had one of the most intimate relationships with God. It is hard for him to grasp the extent of God's anger.

Discipline me, LORD, but only in due measure— not in your anger, or you will reduce me to nothing. (Jeremiah 10:24)

Have you ever disciplined your children in anger – and reduced them to almost nothing? I find it surprising that Jeremiah, often the mouthpiece of God's wrath, fears that God would be angry with him. Perhaps it is because he felt the intensity of God's wrath. The false prophets did not talk much about it. It is not a pleasant topic. When is the last time you heard a sermon on God's wrath?

Who can withstand his indignation? Who can endure his fierce anger? His wrath is poured out like fire; the rocks are shattered before him. (Nahum 1:6)

Sin makes God very angry! And when He is angry, the consequences are often ugly:

Because they have forsaken me and burned incense to other gods and aroused my anger by all that their hands have made, my anger will be poured out on this place and will not be quenched. (2 Chronicles 34:25)

At the breath of God they perish; at the blast of his anger they are no more. (Job 4:9)

He moves mountains without their knowing it and overturns them in his anger. (Job 9:5)

Punishment and judgment

God's anger can result in rebuke or discipline:

LORD, do not rebuke me in your anger or discipline me in your wrath. (Psalm 6:1) Written by David, the man after God's own heart, who also suffered God's discipline after his sin with Bathsheba.

Through your own fault you will lose the inheritance I gave you. I will enslave you to your enemies in a land you do not know, for you have kindled my anger, and it will burn forever. (Jeremiah 17:4)

Perhaps an overstatement because of the depth of God's anger at that point, since we also learn that He is slow to anger, and it is short lived:

But you are a forgiving God, gracious and compassionate, slow to anger and abounding in love. (Nehemiah 9:17)

For his anger lasts only a moment, but his favor lasts a lifetime. (Psalm 30:5)

In a surge of anger I hid my face from you for a moment, but with everlasting kindness I will have compassion on you," says the LORD your Redeemer. (Isaiah 54:8)

It seems that God's anger has to be fully expressed, fully spent, and then will subside:

"Then my anger will cease and my wrath against them will subside, and I will be avenged. And when I have spent my wrath on them, they will know that I the LORD have spoken in my zeal. (Ezekiel 5:13)

Wrath is intense anger, often connected with the outpouring of God's anger at the final judgment:

See, the day of the LORD is coming —a cruel day, with wrath and fierce anger— to make the land desolate and destroy the sinners within it. (Isaiah 13:9)

But because of your stubbornness and your unrepentant heart, you are storing up wrath against yourself for the day of God's wrath, when his righteous judgment will be revealed. (Romans 2:5)

Colossians 3:6 says *because of these [sins], the wrath of God is coming.*

Anger in Revelation

Revelation is full of wrath. Even Jesus, who saves us from the Father's wrath, is angry:

They called to the mountains and the rocks, "Fall on us and hide us from the face of him who sits on the throne and from the wrath of the Lamb! (Revelation 6:16)

A third angel followed them and said in a loud voice: "If anyone worships the beast and its image and receives its mark on their forehead or on their hand, they, too, will drink the wine of God's fury, which has been poured full strength into the cup of his wrath. They will be tormented with burning sulfur in the presence of the holy angels and of the Lamb. And the smoke of their torment will rise for ever and ever. (Revelation 14:9-11)

Those who make a distinction between the Old Testament God of wrath and the New Testament God of love apparently have not read Revelation. The Father did pour out His judgment and wrath on Jesus on the cross, as He bore the penalty for our sin. But far from "growing out" of his anger, God is patiently awaiting the day when He will fully express His wrath.

Apart from Revelation, the New Testament has little "anger", although Jesus was capable of getting angry:

He looked around at them in anger and, deeply distressed at their stubborn hearts, said to the man, "Stretch out your hand." He stretched it out, and his hand was completely restored. (Mark 3:5)

Jesus often expressed anger at the Pharisees, such as in Matthew 23. Probably the best-known example of His anger is casting the moneychangers out of the temple:

Jesus entered the temple courts and drove out all who were buying and selling there. He overturned the tables of the money changers and the benches of those selling doves. (Matthew 21:12)

Several times in His parables, the man representing God becomes angry:

"The servant came back and reported this to his master. Then the owner of the house became angry and ordered his servant, 'Go out quickly into the streets and alleys of the town and bring in the poor, the crippled, the blind and the lame.' (Luke 14:21)

Biblical teaching on managing anger

Moses, David, Samuel, and Nehemiah are all recorded as being angry. However, considering how frequently God's anger is mentioned, there is relatively little scriptural teaching about handling our anger:

Refrain from anger and turn from wrath; do not fret—it leads only to evil. (Psalm 37:8)

Along with other Scriptures, this verse shows that we can control our anger. You can consciously turn away from wrath, turning toward forgiveness or a constructive solution to the problem.

A gentle answer turns away wrath, but a harsh word stirs up anger. (Proverbs 15:1)

We also have the power to turn away other peoples' anger. Our natural tendency is to respond angrily, with harsh words. That will stir up anger, very possibly leading to a full-blown fight. Avoid that. Don't pick fights. A gentle response will tend to shut down the other person's anger. And no, a gentle answer is not unmanly.

Do not make friends with a hot-tempered person, do not associate with one easily angered. (Proverbs 22:24)

We also have choices in the company we keep. Some people are hot-tempered, and we are advised to keep our distance from them. If you associate with others who are easily angered, you will probably find yourself angry and pulled into many situations that will test your commitment to be Christ-like.

Do not be quickly provoked in your spirit, for anger resides in the lap of fools. (Ecclesiastes 7:9)

Anger should be a passing emotion – not residing in your lap. Guard your spirit, since anger begins in your spirit, when something annoys you. Every little thing bothers the fool, but you have the power to choose not to be quickly provoked.

"You have heard that it was said to the people long ago, 'You shall not murder, and anyone who murders will be subject to judgment.' But I tell you that anyone who is angry with a brother or sister will be subject to judgment. Again, anyone who says to a brother or sister, 'Raca,' is answerable to the court. And anyone who says, 'You fool!' will be in danger of the fire of hell. (Matthew 5:21-22)

Anger kills. Anger not dealt with appropriately is as serious as murder and can jeopardize your salvation. Though it might appear that Jesus is saying any anger is wrong, this is a murderous, contemptuous, anger, as conveyed in the words "Raca" and "fool".

"In your anger do not sin". Do not let the sun go down while you are still angry, and do not give the devil a foothold. (Ephesians 4:26-27).

It is easy to sin against someone when we are angry. Unresolved anger can provide a foothold for the devil to destroy relationships, cause us to do something foolish we will later regret, and bring strife into the church. Scripture counsels us not to be quick to anger, but once you are angry, deal with it promptly. Don't let anger simmer for days.

My dear brothers and sisters, take note of this: Everyone should be quick to listen, slow to speak and slow to become angry, because human anger does not produce the righteousness that God desires. (James 1:19-20)

Learning to listen and control your tongue can save you from a lot of anger, strife, and heartache. Anger is not a fruit of the Spirit, and frequently does more harm than good. Practice self-control and don't "fly off the handle."

The Lord looked with favor on Abel and his offering, but on Cain and his offering he did not look with favor. So Cain was very angry, and his face was downcast. Then the Lord said to Cain, "Why are you angry? Why is your face downcast? If you do what is right, will you not be accepted? But if you do not do what is right, sin is crouching at your door; it desires to have you, but you must rule over it." (Genesis 4:4-7)

There is righteous, justified, anger, and there is anger that has no foundation. Cain was angry because he brought God an inferior offering and was not willing to accept correction. We spoke about giving the devil a foothold; here God portrays sin as crouching at the door. Cain still has the ability to rule over it and shut the door. His unjustified anger resulted in murder and drastic consequences for Cain.

So what do we learn about anger?

- It may be the strongest emotion. It can consume and destroy. Anger is a powerful motivator that can cloud our perceptions, but it can also move us to action.

- Much of our problem with anger comes from our lack of self-control and tendency to be quick to anger. God is slow to anger, possibly waiting centuries to express His anger in judgment of sin.

- God gets angry about sin. Though His judgment can be destructive, His purpose is purifying and restoring His people. Our anger can be destructive, and we should not direct it against people, but against the sinful things they do, and the principalities and powers seeking to destroy us.

- God's anger is a very common theme, particularly in the Old Testament. How much have you thought about the possibility that God is angry – even with you? We have yet to see the full extent of His wrath – but it is coming.

- We are made in God's image – and anger is obviously part of His character that we reflect. Anger is good – but sin has twisted it. Be careful not to over-react and reject anger just because it causes trouble in its sinful expressions. Anger has a place in the Christian's life.

- God offers a model of anger that lasts only a moment, balanced by life-long favor. Once you have expressed your anger, let it go and turn your heart toward that person. Choosing to forgive is a good way to put your anger aside.

- God's anger needs to be fully spent – and ours does also. It may be healthier to release much of it at the gym, working at something, or talking to God, and then focus a more manageable portion on the person responsible for your anger.

How to manage your anger

Many self-help books have been written on handling anger, but based on Scripture, I would suggest four steps to help with your anger:

1. Recognize it. Own it. Anger is part of God's image in you. It is not bad. However, when it is out of control (just like sex) it can be very destructive.

- Anger is a warning signal that something is wrong, in a relationship, a situation, or within yourself. Anger is often an expression of deeper emotional struggles, such as depression, shame, grief, loss of control, or fear.

- Take the time to reflect on why you are angry, how you are handling it, and how God wants you to resolve it. It is helpful to write that down in a journal.

- You might ask a Christian brother to keep you accountable, pray with you, and support you as you move to healthier expressions of your anger.

2. Deal decisively with anger from the past, with the anger that can lurk in the corners of our hearts for years. Colossians 3 has instructed us to put it to death.

- We have also seen how that anger can give the devil a foothold. You may have spiritual strongholds that need to be dealt with if anger has been an issue for you. It can be helpful to take some time and write down all the things you are angry about, give each one over to God, and renounce any foothold the enemy has gained through it.

- In some cases, you may still need to resolve that anger by speaking with the person involved. But be aware that resurrecting things the other person forgot can cause more harm. It is often better, with God's help, to forgive them, put the anger to death, and let it go.

3. Study Colossians 3-4 and make it part of your life. Focus on walking in the fullness of the Holy Spirit and putting on the new nature of Christ. Anger is not a fruit of the Spirit. Galatians 5 lists anger in its extreme (fits of rage and related issues) as fruits of our sinful nature. The more you experience your new life in Christ, the less trouble you will have with anger.

4. When you find yourself angry, follow the instructions in 2 Corinthians 10:3-5:

For though we live in the world, we do not wage war as the world does. The weapons we fight with are not the weapons of the world. On the contrary, they have divine power to demolish strongholds. We demolish arguments and every pretension that sets itself up against the knowledge of God, and we take captive every thought to make it obedient to Christ.

- This may be a spiritual battle where Satan could gain a foothold in your life.

- Immediately cry out to Jesus, asking for his help and telling Him how angry you are feeling.

- Step back from the situation and analyze it, seeing how much worldly arguments and pretensions are playing into making you angry.

- Sort out what are legitimate causes of your anger and how much is baggage from other situations. Take those thoughts captive to Christ, prayerfully waiting for wisdom on what steps you may need to take to confront the other person or take action to resolve an unjust situation.

- In your journal, keep track of where you are at with that anger, making sure it is dealt with or put to death, so that it is not harbored in your heart, and potentially an opportunity for the devil to take advantage of you.

God wants to give you victory over destructive anger! Instead of denying it or suppressing it, He wants to teach you how to handle it properly.

15 SEX

I have ministered to thousands of men over the past 40 years: single and married, pastor and prisoner, young and old. Most of them don't talk much about it, but all of them have struggled with sex. Temptations may change as you age, but I have talked with 90-year-old men who still struggle. Sexual sin is a leading cause of pastors' downfalls. Pornography has always been a temptation, but with the internet, it is like a cancer in the church. Some studies say 40% of *pastors* are trapped in internet porn.

We saw in Ephesians 5:3 that a Christian should not even *mention* anything sexually impure or immoral. The sad reality is that many Christian men think and talk about sex all day, and fill their minds with impurity on TV and the internet. It is a tough struggle, but you can overcome this temptation. One of the clearest biblical teachings on sex is found in 1 Corinthians 6:12-20:

> ¹² *"I have the right to do anything," you say—but not everything is beneficial. "I have the right to do anything"—but I will not be mastered by anything.* ¹³ *You say, "Food for the stomach and the stomach for food, and God will destroy them both." The body, however, is not meant for sexual immorality but for the Lord, and the Lord for the body.* ¹⁴ *By his power God raised the Lord from the dead, and he will raise us also.* ¹⁵ *Do you not know that your bodies are members of Christ himself? Shall I*

> then take the members of Christ and unite them
> with a prostitute? Never! [16] Do you not know
> that he who unites himself with a prostitute is
> one with her in body? For it is said, "The two
> will become one flesh." [17] But whoever is united
> with the Lord is one with him in spirit.

> [18] Flee from sexual immorality. All other sins a
> person commits are outside the body, but
> whoever sins sexually, sins against their own
> body. [19] Do you not know that your bodies are
> temples of the Holy Spirit, who is in you, whom
> you have received from God? You are not your
> own; [20] you were bought at a price. Therefore
> honor God with your bodies.

God is very interested in your sex life. After all, it was His idea. He made you a man. Jesus knows what it is like to be a man: He was tempted just like you are – and never sinned. He is your high priest, who is always there to help you (and wants to!). Talk freely with God about your struggles. He already knows about them anyway. Don't separate your spiritual and sexual life.

The Bible talks openly about sex. Song of Solomon celebrates it. In Ephesians 5:31-32 Paul compares the sexual union of a man and woman to the relationship of Christ and the church. The mystery of two people who are one flesh is similar to the mystery of the trinity – three persons in one. That is why Satan has worked overtime to pervert and destroy sex. The Bible chronicles the struggle and failure of many men. Sexual sin was a big problem in Rome and Greece, and it had invaded the church (1 Corinthians 5).

What this passage teaches us:

1. We are free in Christ. Many things are not specifically prohibited, but the question is, are they beneficial? Do they help me be the man God wants me to be? (12)

2. Some things that are permissible can easily master and control us, and then become sin. (12)

3. God made each part of the body for a purpose. Your body is not for you to abuse as you wish. Your body is meant for the Lord, and should be used as He intended. (13)

4. Sex is only for this life – in heaven we will be sex-less, like the angels (see Matthew 22:30). Some might say, "And that's paradise?" But God knows what He is doing.

5. Think carefully about what you are doing with your body, which is a member of Christ. (15)

6. No matter who it is, when you have sex with someone, you become one flesh with them. (16)

7. There is a parallel between the union of a man and woman, and the union of Christ and the believer. (17)

8. We are commanded to flee sexual immorality, and God does not command us to do something without

empowering us to do it. The problem many times is that we don't *want* to flee; we want to jump right in. (18)

9. There is something unique about sexual sin – it touches the deepest part of a man. It is sin against your own body. (18)

10. Your body is a temple of the Holy Spirit. Honor God with your body. (19-20)

11. Jesus bought you with the price of His blood – you are not your own. (19-20)

Some applications of these verses:

1. God's intention is for a man to have one woman for life. That is how we will most fully experience being "one flesh." How is it possible to be "one flesh" with ten women?

   • Any sex outside the committed marital relationship is sin, and robs us of the intimacy God desires us to have with our wives. That includes fantasies, masturbation, and pornography.

   • We know that the Ten Commandments prohibited adultery, and the penalty was death.

   • In this same chapter (verse 9) Paul said that those who continue in sexual sin and adultery cannot be saved.

- Instead of the freedom which some seek in sexual experimentation, sexual sin destroys the power and meaning of the sexual union.

- The best way to show your love to your wife is to come clean of all sexual sin

2. Many men live under great condemnation because they cannot overcome masturbation. It is not the worst sin. Although the Bible never mentions masturbation by name, there are many Biblical principles we can apply to it:

- It is not beneficial. It leaves you empty and far from God.

- It is easy to be mastered by it.

- It stimulates a man to think more about sex, have fantasies, and view pornography.

- God gives wet dreams to provide sexual release, if needed.

- You can live without sex. Christ did. The testimony of many single men, soldiers, prisoners, and others without a wife available, is that life is much easier if you are not constantly stimulated by masturbation, fantasies, and porn.

- Sex is like a fire. Many men are constantly feeding that fire. However, if it is not possible to have sex with your wife, you are better off, especially as a Christian, keeping the fire burning low.

- Think about this as you consider masturbating: Am I honoring God? Do I feel right doing this with a member of Christ?

3. The easy access to porn is lethal. Things arrive uninvited in Emails. And it is not just the internet: TV, magazines...you already know the many things that grab our attention.

- Porn is an addiction. You may need deliverance to get free, or a support group like Celebrate Recovery.

- Do whatever it takes to put appropriate filters on your computer.

- Destroy anything you have, or it will destroy you. Little numbs the spirit like porn.

4. Like Joseph in Egypt, flee from sexual immorality. The moment you start considering temptation and reasoning in your head, you have already lost the battle.

- Memorize and use 1 Corinthians 10:13: *No temptation has overtaken you except what is common to mankind. And God is faithful; he will not let you be tempted beyond what you can bear. But when you are tempted, he will also provide a way out so that you can endure it.* It is possible to win the battle with lust.

- We are not blind. We are going to notice beautiful women, but keep it to one look, and give thanks to God for his beautiful creation. Train your thoughts to stop there.

- Be careful of who you hang out with, and avoid those places (the beach?) where you know you will be tempted.

5. Many men struggle with same-sex attraction. In itself, it is simply a temptation like any of the many temptations that constantly come our way. Don't be surprised at how low the devil goes in bringing crazy thoughts into your mind! Society (even many churches!) increasingly say that homosexuality is normal – even something to celebrate! The Bible is very clear that it is completely contrary to God's plan for us. Don't give the devil a foothold. The fact that you experience these temptations does not mean that you are gay. God wants to help you resist the temptation and overcome the attraction, but be prepared for a struggle.

We are brothers together in this battle! Try to find someone to pray with and keep you accountable. Together we will overcome! Sex is one of the great blessings God has given us, but if you do not follow His divine plan, it can become a curse. My prayer for you is that God would free you from sin, so you can rejoice in the woman God has given you.

16 THE POWER OF THE HOLY SPIRIT

EPHESIANS 4:30 – 5:21

To be Christ-like we must crucify the old man and renew our way of thinking. We identified five areas that should be transformed in chapter 13. How is it going for you? I am sure you already know how hard it is to be like Christ, but I have good news for you: God Himself wants to live inside you, giving you the power to obey Him, overcome sin, and walk with Jesus.

- Are you experiencing that power?
- Are you full of the Holy Spirit?
- Do you want to experience more of the Spirit?

Hidden in this long passage (Ephesians 4:17 - 5:21) are four keys to experiencing the Spirit's power:

1. Do not grieve the Spirit (4:30).
2. Cultivate the fruit of the Spirit (5:9).
3. Walk in the light (5:11).
4. Be filled – even drunk! – with the Spirit (5:18).

Do not grieve the Holy Spirit

4:30 *And do not grieve the Holy Spirit of God, with whom you were sealed for the day of redemption.* (NIV)

The Holy Spirit is a person: the third person of the trinity.

- He has feelings.
- He loves you.
- His purpose is to conform you to the image of Christ and help you walk in a way that pleases God.

Sadly, often in ignorance, we grieve the Spirit. And like any person who has been hurt or offended, after a while He backs away, and you no longer feel his presence or power. Your heart is empty.

Decide now to do whatever you can to avoid grieving him. Carefully think about what you do. If you are sensitive to the Spirit, you will know when He is grieved. All the works of the flesh we have looked at in this passage, all sin, grieve Him. Is it possible you are not feeling His presence because you have quenched him and grieved him?

The Spirit also sealed you for the day when Christ returns. He marked you as God's property, giving you assurance of your salvation and the hope of heaven.

Cultivate the fruit of the Spirit

5:7 Therefore do not be partners with [the disobedient sons of darkness]. 8 For you were once darkness, but now you are light in the Lord. Live as children of light 9 (for the fruit of the light consists in all goodness, righteousness and truth) 10 and find out what pleases the Lord.

We all walked in darkness, along with others who were just as sinful and lost. If you keep walking with them, you will stay in the dark. To follow Jesus you have to leave them, and walk in the light with others who love Jesus. Of course, you can tell them about Christ, but if you want the fullness of the Spirit, you cannot take part in their lifestyle. They may even feel uncomfortable around you; since you are in the light, their sin is exposed.

Something is wrong if you do not feel a deep desire to please God. Carefully evaluate everything you do in light of the Word, to see if it is pleasing to Him. If the Spirit is present in your life, His fruit should be evident. Here it mentions goodness, righteousness, and truth. Galatians 5 adds the fruits of love, joy, peace, forbearance, kindness, faithfulness, gentleness and self-control, and lists the fruit of the sinful nature (verses 19-21): *sexual immorality, impurity and debauchery; idolatry and witchcraft; hatred, discord, jealousy, fits of rage, selfish ambition, dissensions, factions and envy; drunkenness, orgies, and the like.*

You will know them by their fruit. What is the fruit of your life?

- Do people you spend time with demonstrate fruit of the Spirit? Or of the flesh?
- Are you walking in darkness or light?
- Are there things you feel you need to hide from your wife or your pastor?
- Is your light shining before others?
- When you enter a room, do you bring the presence of Christ with you?

Lacking fruit of the Spirit is a warning that something is wrong. You are probably quenching the Spirit because you spend most of the day in darkness. Ten minutes of devotions, listening to

Christian music, and spending a few hours each week in church does not counteract hours in the dark.

To experience the Sprit's fullness, walk in the light

11 Have nothing to do with the fruitless deeds of darkness, but rather expose them. 12 It is shameful even to mention what the disobedient do in secret. 13 But everything exposed by the light becomes visible—and everything that is illuminated becomes a light. 14 This is why it is said:

"Wake up, sleeper,
  rise from the dead,
  and Christ will shine on you."

Take no part in and have no fellowship with the fruitless deeds and enterprises of darkness, but instead [let your lives be so in contrast as to] expose and reprove and convict them. For it is a shame even to speak of or mention the things that [such people] practice in secret. But when anything is exposed and reproved by the light, it is made visible and clear; and where everything is visible and clear there is light. (AMP)

You should shun the darkness to the extent that you do not even *talk* about the shameful things done in secret. Rather, your light exposes them. Even more, we are to *reprove* (or *rebuke*) them. Rebuking sounds harsh. You may be concerned about offending someone, but it is the *deeds* of darkness we reprove, not the people. True, that is still very "politically incorrect," and we need to be sensitive in the way we go about it. The rebuking may be done in prayer, but do not be afraid to reprove them! These deeds of darkness are diabolical, and part of our spiritual battle. They are fruitless! Where do they lead? Pregnancy? Jail? Death? Sickness?

We must be very careful here: We are commanded not to even *mention* these things! Yet I observe a *fascination* with them, even among Christians! How can you watch movies full of the deeds of darkness, which even glorify them? How can you take part in off-color jokes? Or indulge in internet sites you have no business visiting? I have heard people rationalize: "You can't hide from the world. We need to be aware of what they're into." Garbage! We are only too aware of what sin is all about! And there is certainly no need to add more vivid details to what we already know! If you want the power of the Spirit, wake up and let the light of Christ shine in your heart!

[15] Be very careful, then, how you live—not as unwise but as wise, [16] making the most of every opportunity, because the days are evil.

A few minutes on the internet or watching the news confirms it: the days are evil. We have to be super vigilant about how we live. You cannot go on autopilot, assuming that life is basically good. Make the most of every moment God gives you. How? With video games? On the internet? Watching TV? Get wise about how you live and spend your time!

Be filled with the Spirit

[17] Therefore do not be foolish, but understand what the Lord's will is. [18] Do not get drunk on wine, which leads to debauchery. Instead, be filled with the Spirit, [19] speaking to one another with psalms, hymns, and songs from the Spirit. Sing and make music

from your heart to the Lord, [20] always giving thanks to God the Father for everything, in the name of our Lord Jesus Christ.

Don't act thoughtlessly, but understand what the Lord wants you to do. Don't be drunk with wine, because that will ruin your life. (NLT)

There are two things mentioned here which quench the Spirit and ruin your life:

- Abusing alcohol and drugs. God says they lead to debauchery: a life of depraved self-indulgence. I found something very odd as I looked up the word debauchery: It is currently in the top 1% of lookups, and is the 229th most popular word on Merriam-Webster.com! Maybe that is an indication of where our culture is? The definition given there is "Bad or immoral behavior that involves sex, drugs, alcohol, etc. Extreme indulgence in sensuality. Seduction from virtue or duty (archaic)." If you have problems with alcohol or drugs, get help! God wants to free you from that addiction! Get to Alcoholics Anonymous or Celebrate Recovery, or it will ruin your life!

- Acting foolishly. Often we do not realize what we are doing. We are in a hurry and act impulsively, without thinking about the consequences. Intelligent men do stupid things. Seek God and listen for the Spirit's guidance. He wants to direct your steps and help you avoid foolish mistakes.

These things help the Spirit flow in your life:

- Doing God's will. Understand what it is, study to learn about it, and, especially, do it. Disobedience quenches the Spirit, but He empowers the person who truly wants to please God and do his will.

- Similar to the way a drunk is controlled by his alcohol or addicted to his drug, we are commanded to be filled with the Spirit. Jesus spoke of drinking of the Spirit (John 7:37-39). Get into His presence and drink. The Spirit is a gentleman – He will not force His way into your life, but waits for a hungry and open heart. Let the Spirit fill you. Give Him freedom. Do not resist Him.

- Worship the Lord with other believers. The Spirit loves to lift up Jesus, and is very present when God's people are together worshipping Him.

- Fill your heart with worship throughout the day. Listening to worship music on your iPod or on the radio is not the same as singing to the Lord. We are so constantly bombarded by noise, I notice very few people singing anymore! And often our worship songs are so complex it is hard to memorize them! Learn how to sing to the Lord in your heart throughout the day.

- Give thanks to God in *everything*. Cultivate an attitude of gratitude. Grumbling and complaining quenches the Spirit. Thanksgiving recognizes His presence and your belief that He really is good.

The Spirit-filled person is joyful: singing, and praising, and thanking God. The Spirit impacts his whole life. Do you want to be filled with the Spirit? Give your life to Jesus as your Lord. Confess any sin and ask his forgiveness, and ask God to fill you with His Spirit: *"If you then, though you are evil, know how to give good gifts to your children, how much more will your Father in heaven give the Holy Spirit to those who ask him!"* (Luke 11:13)

The bridge to the next step

²¹ *Submit to one another out of reverence for Christ.*

This verse is a bridge to the third step on the road to mature manhood. It does not come naturally. In the world, it just does not work. The old man wants to be in charge, but in the Spirit, we submit to each other. Consciously decide to submit to your wife (yes, even her!), your boss, and whoever you meet during the day. Especially submit to brothers and sisters in Christ. Do not force your own will on others. There is actually tremendous freedom here! You don't have to prove yourself or lift yourself up!

This ends the process that began with commitment to a local church. It is almost impossible in your own strength, but with a renewed mind and crucified flesh, you can trust God and submit to others. Then God can fill you with the power of His Spirit. Only when you learn to submit to others and humble yourself will you have the attitude necessary for an intimate relationship. You will be ready for marriage. Without the foundation of the church as the first step, and a life transformed by the power of the Spirit in this second step, you will have problems in your marriage. Are you ready to have your relationships transformed?

THIRD STEP:

MARRIAGE, FAMILY, AND WORK

17 MARRIAGE

EPHESIANS 5:21–33

Are you like many men? Do you open a book on marriage and go straight to the chapter on sex? A lot of us would like to skip the hard work and get straight to the fun part. Did you ever wonder why sex is always buried toward the back of the book? I have never seen it as the first chapter. A great sex life requires a solid foundation in other areas of your marriage.

In these four steps, the foundation (your participation in a healthy church) is essential for the transformation of your sinful nature, and it is a huge help to have the mind of Christ in your family relationships. Remember, the steps build on each other, and each needs to be maintained. It is not as if you complete one step and have everything down, so you just move on to the next step. In fact, there is nothing like marriage to reveal the depths of your selfishness and sin, and your need for the Holy Spirit. And the support of caring brothers in Christ will help you through the inevitable marital struggles.

I know I am entering holy ground here: a man's home is his castle. Most men feel like no one has the right to tell them how to act in their own home. It is very touchy to talk about things that are so close to our hearts, but it is important to be open to the Spirit of God and put our homes in order, according to the Word of God.

I have known many men very involved in their churches – even pastors! – who seem to be models of a holy life: No offensive habits and exemplary self-discipline. They have done a great job on the first two steps to mature manhood, but unfortunately, their progress stopped there. Talk to their wives or kids; their family life is a nightmare. Rigid legalism crowds out Christ's love, and forget about mercy. Yet you cannot reach true maturity as a man if your family and sexuality are not in order.

So, we have finally made it to the third step! Are you ready for marriage? I have been married 34 years and I am still not sure if I am ready! Of course, I thought I was ready when I got married – especially for physical intimacy. I had even written and taught a course called *Preparing for Marriage*. If we wait until we have everything together to get married, we probably would all be single! If you are single, there are principles here that apply to any relationship, but this may just be God's way of giving you the right mindset for that special woman he has waiting for you.

As we enter this holy sanctuary of the home, we may need to repent. Even the most committed men of God often neglect their marriages, and lack love and forgiveness. Or, worse, actually abuse their wives or children (physically, sexually, or emotionally). We also need to enter the home with a humble, teachable spirit. God has a plan for the family. If we do things our way, following the world, or even our parents' example, our marriages will probably suffer. We have to separate our culture and family history from the revelation of God's will in the Bible.

Submit to one another

We enter marriage, then, with the verse that serves as a bridge from the second step (5:21):

Submit to one another out of reverence for Christ.

Submission. This one word applies to all relationships. First, submission to Christ's lordship. By nature we are rebels, but rebellion is like the sin of witchcraft (1 Samuel 15:23). We have to submit to God. That same attitude is necessary in the church, where we submit to the authority of the Bible, the pastor, and other leaders. This submissive heart should impact our whole life. Some people are very submissive in church, but rebels at home. The command applies to every relationship. Yes, even the husband submitting to his wife. That calls for humility and Christ's attitude, which we see in Philippians 2:5-8:

In your relationships with one another, have the same mindset as Christ Jesus:

Who, being in very nature God,
*   did not consider equality with God something to be used to*
his own advantage;
rather, he made himself nothing
*   by taking the very nature of a servant,*
*   being made in human likeness.*
And being found in appearance as a man,
*   he humbled himself*
*   by becoming obedient to death—*
*   even death on a cross!*

Do you have Christ's mindset? Can you see how it is almost impossible in the flesh? Submission will only work in the context of Ephesians 4:18-20: drunk on the Spirit. We do not do this out of fear of our wives, but out of fear of God, recognizing that He commands us to submit. We do it in obedience, following Jesus' example, and out of reverence for him.

Many men, especially Christian men, enter marriage ready to rule their homes. They want to be served by their wives. By nature, we are prideful and selfish. Learning to humble ourselves and submit to others, out of reverence for Christ, and trusting that He wants what is best for you and your family, will do a lot for your marriage. As we will see, it is true that man is the head, but that also gives us the freedom to submit to our wives at times – out of love. You may be head *of your family*, my brother, but you are not *the* head. Christ is. If you are not submitted to His lordship, if Christ is not truly the head of your home, your marriage will struggle. If you or your wife are walking in darkness, your home will be dark. Your children will suffer, and be oppressed by that darkness. If your family is isolated from the support and ministry of the church, you will be like those children that are tossed about on the waves, constantly up and down. But if you are filled with the Spirit and growing in a good church, your whole family will be blessed.

God's plan for wives

²² *Wives, submit yourselves to your own husbands as you do to the Lord.* ²³ *For the husband is the head of the wife as Christ is the head of the church, his body, of which he is the Savior.* ²⁴ *Now as the church submits to Christ, so also wives should submit to their husbands in everything.*

New translations say *submit*, because the Greek word Paul used, *be subject*, sounds too strong. Unfortunately, submit has just as negative a connotation to many women, especially if their husband is abusive. Yet their sin does not negate the truth, or the need to obey it. As with everything in God's plan, the devil will do his best to pervert it.

What it means to submit

1. The wife must be subject to her husband *as to the Lord*. If she is not submitted to Jesus, it will be hard for her to submit to her husband. If she has learned to trust in Jesus and be subject to Him, it will be easier in the marriage.

2. The other model of submission is the church's submission to Christ. Few would argue that Christ needs to rule in His church. We are His body and we must obey Him. *In that same way*, the wife must submit to her husband.

3. The submission is *in everything*: in the church, for both men and women, and in the home, for the wife. It is not for us to choose what we will obey from the Scripture, or whether we like it or not. And it is not for the woman to decide if she will obey something or not: the example and the command is *in everything*.

4. There is order in the Kingdom of God. Everyone needs a head. The head of the church is Christ, who is also the head of every man. The head of a married woman is her husband.

5. The husband/wife relationship is a reflection of Christ and His church. He died for our salvation. We are His presence in the world. I have heard many explanations of how *head* means *source*, in an attempt to tone down what Paul says and defend an egalitarian marriage. This is not a scholarly study, but all it takes is common sense: Your head, your brain, directs all your bodily function. The head of an organization is in charge of everything that group does. As head of the church, Christ has total authority and directs everything it does. In the same way, the husband clearly has authority and responsibility as head of his home.

6. But that doesn't give him unlimited power, nor is it a matter of superiority or inferiority. It is the heart attitude of a humble woman who loves the Lord and her husband.

7. Christ is obviously our only Savior. But Paul mentions his role as Savior of His church, referring to the husband's self-sacrifice and participation in his wife's sanctification, which will be explained in the following verses.

The wife must respect her husband

The only other instruction for wives is in verse 33: *the wife must respect her husband.*

Look at how the Amplified Bible clarifies that! *Let the wife see that she respects and reverences her husband [that she notices him, regards him, honors him, prefers him, venerates, and esteems him; and that she defers to him, praises him, and loves and admires him exceedingly].*

Isn't there something that jumps in your heart as you read that, men? More than slavish submission, isn't that what you really long for from your wife? Obviously, it doesn't mean she praises you as we praise the Lord, but we do thrive on her praise (instead of criticism). Some women may fear it will only make us more prideful, but if you truly love her and are obedient to the command for *you* to have a submissive attitude, that honor and respect is the support you desperately need. And you, my brother, need to walk worthy of your calling and of her respect. If we are honest, many of us have made it very hard for her to respect us!

God's plan for husbands

[25]Husbands, love your wives, just as Christ loved the church and gave himself up for her.

Which is easier? Being a believer? Or being Christ? Sure, Jesus has the power and authority, but that comes with a price. Like suffering on the cross, and supplying us with everything we need. All we have to do is accept the gift of salvation and walk with Him.

The Greek word used here for love is *agape*, the unconditional love God has for us. Once again, Christ is our model for marriage. If you need guidance on being a husband, study how Christ related to people. Was He hard on them? Only the hypocrites. With "sinners," the sick, and the common people He was very compassionate. And Jesus said the head, the leader, must be a servant. Many men want their wives to serve *them*, but we are the ones who need to serve our wives.

Yes, I think much more is demanded of the husband than the wife. Jesus laid down His life and denied himself for us. The husband has to sacrifice himself for his wife; lay down your own desires and die to self for her wellbeing, always thinking about her before yourself. The emphasis for the man is not authority, but loving service.

So what does it mean to love your wife? I'm guessing you have already discovered you do not have it in you to love like Christ. His power in you enables you to be Christ-like and loving. We may think we are great lovers, but my observation is that most men know very little about really loving a woman. It is way more than good performance in the bedroom. Christ took the initiative in loving us, and it is our responsibility as men to do the same. She is designed to respond to that love with a willing submission. We do not demand her submission – that is something she has to settle with the Lord. Paul does not talk about the woman *loving* her husband – although clearly she should. Submitting and respecting him is what is hardest for her. It is easy for the man to take charge in the home – that is our nature. However, love sometimes means submitting to her desires. What is hard for men is overcoming our natural self-centeredness and laying down our lives for her.

My brother, are you ready to sacrifice everything for your wife? Is her happiness of first importance to you?

²⁶ *So that He might sanctify her, having cleansed her by the washing of water with the Word,* ²⁷ *That He might present the*

church to Himself in glorious splendor, without spot or wrinkle or any such things, that she might be holy and faultless. (AMP)

Do you have a vision for your wife?

We are talking here about what Christ did for us – but also what a husband should do for his wife. Christ has a clear vision for His church – and is hard at work conforming us to that vision. Do you have a vision for your wife? For your kids? For your family? I'm not talking about some vision of her as a beauty queen. When you came to Christ, were you already clean and looking good? No! You were dirty and broken, but Christ had a vision of what you were designed to be and what you could be. Right now your wife may be tired, and a long way from that glorious vision – but meditate on what Christ wants for her, pray over her, and have faith that God will work with you to bring that vision to reality. Ask God to give you a vision for her that is based on the Word. What is God's purpose for her? What is her calling?

Sanctify her as Christ sanctifies the church

Christ sanctifies us; cleans us up and gets us away from destructive things. How? By washing us in His blood and His Word. Do you want a holy wife? Minister the Word to her. Do everything in your power to help her walk in holiness. Amazingly, some Christian men do not want their wives to be *too* holy. It is almost as if we fear losing them to Christ!

Jesus is working on a glorious bride for Himself. After all His work and sacrifice, He wants a spotless, faultless church, of glorious splendor. And it is your responsibility to work to present your wife to Christ the same way. Are you aware, my brother, that someday you are going to give an account to your Lord, face to face? You might tell Him "Look at this great ministry I raised up and the beautiful building they have." And the Lord may say to you "That's very nice, but I want to see your wife. Bring her to me." Will you be ashamed on that day? Or will you come joyfully and confidently, and present your radiant bride to Christ? Will it be evident how much she has benefited from your loving care? What a great sin to answer for if you have abused this treasure physically or with your words.

28 In the same way, husbands ought to love their wives as they love their own bodies. For a man who loves his wife actually shows love for himself. 29 No one hates his own body but feeds and cares for it, just as Christ cares for the church. 30 And we are members of his body. 33 So again I say, each man must love his wife as he loves himself. (NLT)

Happy wife, happy life

It sounds trite. It seems like our happiness should come from Christ, and not be wrapped up with our wives. But I have had countless men confirm what I have also found to be true, and these verses tell us why: We are one flesh. Everything that affects your wife affects you. What a shame that some men wear the latest fashions and spend hours working out and taking care of their own bodies – but neglect their wives.

The best thing you can do for yourself is love and care for your wife. If you neglect her, you are neglecting yourself. There are many sick marriages, which men simply have not cared for. Sadly, the wife is often more concerned for the state of the marriage than the man, who can be blissfully unaware of problems in the marriage - until the woman walks out or has an affair. As a man, make your marriage a priority. Be sure she gets your emotional support. Many men provide money, food, and other necessities - and think they have done their job. Meanwhile their wives are starving for their attention and affection.

Look at how intimate Christ's relationship is to us: We are members of His body! That is a picture of marriage as well! This is something so spiritual and holy that we can never achieve it with our own efforts. It should show the world the nature of Christ's relationship to the church! No wonder Satan is so intent on destroying it!

There is great security here. That is why marriage is so important in a day when it is under attack from all directions. It is not just the legal aspect, but honoring the Lord, and confirming your commitment to your wife before him and his body, the church.

A great mystery: One flesh

[31] *"For this reason a man will leave his father and mother and be united to his wife, and the two will become one flesh."* [32] *This is a profound mystery—but I am talking about Christ and the church.*

Indeed, we are treading on holy ground here. Paul calls this a profound mystery. Just like we cannot fully understand the Trinity or how we can be united to Christ, it is impossible to comprehend the intimacy of a husband and wife. Maybe you already know that your wife and your marriage are mysteries – beyond your understanding! The man will be united to his wife and they will be one flesh. We like that one flesh part – and it makes sex something intensely spiritual and beautiful. But it goes beyond sex and should involve an emotional and spiritual bonding. Jesus said that no man should separate what God has joined together. How is it possible to be one flesh with multiple women? Marriage is for life! God hates divorce! It breaks His heart!

It is the man who is called to leave his parents. Did you know that many men have never left mommy? Of course, we will always love our mothers, but both your wife and your mother need to know that your wife has first place in your life. You have your own home and family now. If you always give preference to your mother, you will destroy your marriage. Your wife also needs to leave her family. It can be a huge problem if she is too close to her mother.

Remember – all this calls for the anointing of the Holy Spirit, empowering you to love and be Christ-like. Give church its proper place, but don't let it overwhelm your marriage. Some men escape to the church to avoid their duties as husbands. And do not get jealous of appropriate time your wife spends at church. Work together and seek God to determine how He wants church to be part of your lives.

Isn't God's plan for marriage amazing? It is not easy, and I have not known many couples who really have a handle on it. Too many want to adjust God's plan to suit themselves or our culture. But do you have faith that God knows what He is talking about? Do you have faith it could work in your marriage? Start loving your wife in a Christ-like way. Put aside your own desires and lay down your life for her. The submission and respect parts (and the sexual intimacy) will take care of themselves. God's power will be released to make your marriage more than you ever dreamed possible.

18   YOUR FAMILY AND WORK

EPHESIANS 6:1–9

Your children need a family of faith to train them in God's ways. Not just your home, although a Christian home is crucial, but a healthy church functioning according to God's plan as revealed in Ephesians 4. That experience should establish church as a life-long, integral part of their lives. Children in a legalistic church full of hypocrisy are much more apt to reject the church – and Christ – as teenagers. This foundation of the church should have been established in your first step to mature manhood.

Next, the example of an honest, godly father in a living relationship with Jesus will have a huge impact on your kids. And you need the power of the Holy Spirit to discern God's will for your family, and to wisely lead them.

After that relationship with Jesus, the most important thing you can do for your kids is love their mother according to the word we just studied in Ephesians 5. Children need the security of a father who loves mom, and a mother who honors dad. If the wife is rebellious or manipulative, her children will follow her example. A good marriage is the essential foundation as you move through this third step. It will guard your children from the devastation of divorce, and help you resist the temptation of pornography or an affair.

Instructions to children

[1]Children, obey your parents in the Lord, for this is right. [2]"Honor your father and mother"—which is the first commandment with a promise— [3]"so that it may go well with you and that you may enjoy long life on the earth."

Children, obey your parents in the Lord [as His representatives], for this is just and right. Honor (esteem and value as precious) your father and your mother... (AMP)

Submission is also the key word for children — but here Paul makes it a little stronger, and uses the word *obey*, which he did not use for the wife. More than just a submissive, honoring, attitude, children are required to obey their parents. It is the right thing — and *righteous* thing — to do. He does give one caveat — it is *in the Lord*. That does not justify disobeying non-Christian parents — in fact it may be even more important to obey them, as a testimony. But children are not obligated to obey their parents if it means disobeying God, although young children may not have that option, or even know what it is they are to obey.

Adult children are not required to be subordinate to domineering parents — although they still need to honor (love and respect) them. It is possible to obey without honor. It is also right to honor the elderly in general — something that we are losing today.

The parent-child relationship is very important to God. After all, He is our Father, and we are His children! Your home should reflect that relationship! It is also one of the Ten Commandments. God promises a long, blessed life if you honor your parents. Under the Law, a child who cursed his parents was put to death (Leviticus 20:9). There would be many dead children today if we still obeyed that command! Rebellious kids are a huge problem – but parents bear much of the blame.

Instructions to Fathers

⁴ Fathers, do not exasperate your children; instead, bring them up in the training and instruction of the Lord.

Fathers, do not irritate and provoke your children to anger [do not exasperate them to resentment], but rear them [tenderly] in the training and discipline and the counsel and admonition of the Lord. (AMP)

- Don't provoke your children to anger.
- Don't irritate or exasperate them.
- Don't push them to the point that they resent you.
- Don't put too high expectations on them, and don't be harsh with them.

Instead, focus on forming them into men and women of God. Be careful of disciplining them in frustration or anger. They need your counsel and wisdom. A good relationship is probably more important than perfect behavior.

I have to confess: I used to enjoy provoking and irritating my son, kind of like I enjoy provoking my dog. It is something I have observed in many fathers; it may be a way of relating man to man. It is our way of toughening them up. The truth is, many of us don't know how to relate very well to our kids. Here again it is the church's responsibility to provide orientation and support. In most churches, there are few opportunities for fathers to get together and share their concerns, failures, and successes in fathering, and pray for each other. When women get together, their children are a focus of conversation, but men rarely talk about their kids with other men. Take the risk and initiate a conversation with a brother in Christ, or your dad, or your own brother. It can really help. Read books. Talk with your wife about her experiences and fears as a mother, and your feelings about fathering. Pray with her for your children.

They need you. You do not have to be an expert. We are all learning. More than anything, they want your time and attention. Do not leave all the discipline to your wife. Sit down with her and come up with a plan of discipline both of you can follow – and stick with it. Have daily family devotions, and teach them God's Word, as commanded in the great *Shema* of Deuteronomy 6:4-9:

> *Hear, O Israel: The Lord our God, the Lord is one. Love the Lord your God with all your heart and with all your soul and with all your strength. These commandments that I give you today are to be on your hearts. Impress them on your children. Talk about them when you sit at home and when you walk along the road, when you lie down and when you get up. Tie them as symbols on your hands and bind them on your foreheads. Write them on the doorframes of your houses and on your gates.*

It is interesting that Paul has nothing to say to mothers. I suspect that if the man does his part, the woman naturally assumes her part as mother.

Prospering on the job

[5] Slaves, obey your earthly masters with respect and fear, and with sincerity of heart, just as you would obey Christ. [6] Obey them not only to win their favor when their eye is on you, but as slaves of Christ, doing the will of God from your heart. [7] Serve wholeheartedly, as if you were serving the Lord, not people, [8] because you know that the Lord will reward each one for whatever good they do, whether they are slave or free.

Slaves, obey your earthly masters with deep respect and fear. Serve them sincerely as you would serve Christ. [6] Try to please them all the time, not just when they are watching you. As slaves of Christ, do the will of God with all your heart. [7] Work with enthusiasm, as though you were working for the Lord rather than for people. [8] Remember that the Lord will reward each one of us for the good we do, whether we are slaves or free. (NLT)

Some translations say *servants*, but the word usually means *slave*. The sad reality is that slavery was common in that day, and Christians had slaves, as we see in the book of Philemon. The point here is not to condone or condemn the institution of slavery. The early church did not prohibit believers from having slaves, or encourage slaves to run away or rebel. What we have here are principles that apply to anyone on their job. There are many testimonies of God prospering those who follow this counsel. That is why many employers choose to hire Christians: They know they are good workers who do not drink or steal.

- Here again a submissive and respectful attitude is most important. Obey your boss with respect and sincerity.

Obey him as you would Christ, enthusiastically and whole-heartedly.

- You are already Christ's slave. Bring that same attitude to your job, which is a training ground to learn servanthood and display the fruit of the Spirit.
- Work as though it were for Jesus. He knows everything you do on the job. I am amazed at how much time is wasted today on the internet and smart phones. That is stealing time from your employer. Serve your boss – no matter how bad he may be – as if you were serving Christ.
- You may feel your pay is not fair, and it may not be. But your real pay – your reward – is from God. That is far better than whatever you earn now. God knows the work you do and gives you a totally fair evaluation.

How are you measuring up? Trust Him to lift you up and free you from your slavery or hard labor in due time. If you are unemployed, trust Him to provide you with work. And thank Him for the job you have and the opportunity to serve Him there.

God will bless you for your hard work and the glory you bring to His name. Ask Him what He wants you doing, and if He might have a job change for you. Are you truly using your talents? Are you in an honest job that really helps people? Has God put a desire in your heart for another job? Should you take classes to prepare for it? It can feel intimidating to look for another job, but it may be God's will for you.

Masters

⁹ And masters, treat your slaves in the same way. Do not threaten them, since you know that he who is both their Master and yours is in heaven, and there is no favoritism with him.

You masters, act on the same [principle] toward them and give up threatening and using violent and abusive words, knowing that He Who is both their Master and yours is in heaven, and that there is no respect of persons (no partiality) with Him. (AMP)

God is no respecter of persons; He does not have favorites. You may be a big shot on your job, overseeing many people and a big budget, but in God's eyes, you are just the same as the janitor: We are all equal before God. The only difference is God holds you accountable for what you have been given. If He has given you more talent and responsibility, you will have to answer for how you use it, and how you have treated those under you (just like a husband has a greater accountability for how he has treated his wife and children). Read verses 5-8 on servants again. The same guidelines about working for Christ and receiving your real reward from Him apply here. Be very careful how you treat those under you. You have the privilege of modeling Jesus to them. Make sure they can see Christ in you. In the past, corporate leaders (like Henry Ford and George Eastman of Kodak) took a genuine interest in their employees, their families, and the community. Today the employee is often the last one considered. Everything is about making more money and boosting the stock. Be different – take genuine interest in your employees.

Work and family take up most of the time in a man's life. If you fail to apply God's Word here, you will never arrive at mature manhood. This is where things can get rough. This third step is not easy, but if you do not have your work and family lined up with God's will, you will be very vulnerable in the warfare that is part of the fourth step on the way to maturity.

THE FOURTH STEP:

VICTORY IN THE SPIRITUAL BATTLE

19　War!

For thousands of years, men have left their families and gone off to war. Many never returned home. I am grateful that I was too young to fight in Vietnam, and never had that experience of warfare. My father served in the Second World War, in Australia, and always said it made him a man. I am sure there is truth in that. We have become very comfortable and lazy; it's fine to fight enemies in video games, but forget about suffering in a real war. Yet for this final step to mature manhood, we have to leave the comforts of home for the battlefield (even though, unfortunately, some homes are also battlefields!). We have to leave the innocence of childhood and acknowledge that we are in a war. Whether that battle is at home, or with the forces of evil in the world, God wants to train and prepare you.

It makes a lot of sense that this last step to mature manhood is at the end of Ephesians. You need some maturity to go to war. Remember when Israel left Egypt? God sent them on a longer route through the desert, because He knew they weren't ready for battle.

We have already looked at three important ways God prepares us:

- The first step is being part of a healthy church where gifts and ministries are functioning. The solitary

183

Christian is a target for the devil. Your pastor and the Body of Christ offer great protection against his attacks.

- Next, we must walk in holiness. I cannot tell you how many times I have heard about someone suffering under the devil's attacks. Life is a struggle. But they spend all day listening to worldly music. They fill their minds with TV and movies. They go places on the internet no Christian should go. Most of their friends are non-Christian. Of course the devil is going to have a field day with them!

- The third step is getting your family in order. A strong marriage keeps you free from many temptations. Your family is very important to your spiritual health. When pastors stumble, it is often with another woman or pornography.

If these three areas are in order, you are well on your way to victory and maturity. But you are still in a war, and you need armor and weapons, which brings us to Ephesians 6.

Be strong in the Lord

10 Finally, be strong in the Lord and in his mighty power.

In conclusion, be strong in the Lord [be empowered through your union with Him]; draw your strength from Him [that strength which His boundless might provides]. (AMP)

Do you know any man who wants to be weak? Of course not! We all want to be strong! But this is not strength you get by working out. This strength only comes from the Lord; it is His mighty, unlimited, power, which Paul spoke about in chapter 3.

How do you strengthen yourself, or draw strength from Christ? The same way you get strong physically: In the gym, lifting weights, and eating right. Get busy with the things of God. Exercise your faith. Carry those heavy burdens. The Lord is increasing the weight to make you stronger. Feast on God's Word.

Sadly, you can be in a great church, have your family in order, and walk in the light – but still be a weakling in the Lord. It is time to work those spiritual muscles. God wants you strong.

Put your armor on

[11] Put on the full armor of God, so that you can take your stand against the devil's schemes.

Put on God's whole armor [the armor of a heavy-armed soldier which God supplies], that you may be able successfully to stand up against [all] the strategies and the deceits of the devil. (AMP)

The devil is attacking you right now. If you do not have your armor on, you are vulnerable. You will be like that child tossed back and forth on the waves, with constant ups and downs. There is no rest in this battle. You don't leave home in your underwear, do you? Well, don't start the day without your spiritual armor. You need it every day.

The Bible does not instruct us to pick a fight with Satan or go looking for him. Jesus did not seek out demonized people. In fact, He told them to be quiet. Paul did not look for fights with Satan. Be careful of people who want to go and fight the devil; God does not need cowboys who show off how tough they are. It may look good on TV, but you are playing with fire. When the devil comes (and he will), resist him, and use your armor. Then you can rebuke him in Jesus' name.

Perhaps most important, if you are walking in the light, in a good church, and full of the Spirit, it will be hard for the devil to touch you. The command here is to stand firm and resist him, strong and secure in your identity in Christ. You are seated with Christ in heavenly places, already in a position of power and authority. Jesus defeated the devil on the cross. You just need to hold your ground.

Many neglect their relationship with God. The devil has no mercy; he is always watching you, just waiting for that day you are a little weak, or you do not go to church. When you are sick or tired, when a few days have gone by without fellowship with the Lord, or your faith is wavering, be careful! He is like a roaring lion looking for someone to devour!

Do you know about his evil, deceitful, strategies and schemes? Do you realize he is determined to destroy you and your family? Wake up! Learn to recognize how he works. Strengthen yourself in the Lord and in his power, and get ready for battle!

My God, thank you that I am seated in heavenly places, in a position of authority. I have authority over the enemy because I am in Christ and Christ is in me. I stand firm on your Word, the blood of Jesus, and His victory on the cross. Thank you that I am more than a conqueror in Christ. In Jesus' name, Amen.

20 THE TRUE NATURE OF THE BATTLE
EPHESIANS 6:12-13

¹² For we are not fighting against flesh-and-blood enemies, but against evil rulers and authorities of the unseen world, against mighty powers in this dark world, and against evil spirits in the heavenly places. (NLT)

This is where the battle really is at. Like it or not, you are in the middle of a war. If you are walking in the flesh, you are going to fight in the flesh. But this is a spiritual battle, which we have to fight with spiritual weapons, following our Commander in Chief, Jesus Christ, according to the battle plan revealed in the Bible. A key part of that plan, which is often overlooked, is the importance of the church. You are part of a great army. It is very dangerous to go into battle alone.

Satan comes to us as an angel of light; a wolf dressed like a meek lamb. Open your eyes! Your enemy is not your wife, your boss, or your mother-in-law. The devil's deception leads to fighting other people. There is a spiritual, invisible, world of principalities, powers, and spiritual forces in heavenly places, better known as demons. They appear to be well organized as an army under Satan's control, with principalities assigned over nations, cities, and families. Pray for the discernment to know what principalities you are fighting. Name them if you can, and take authority over them in Jesus' Name. Be careful of taking on too much; when you start battling a major principality, the backlash can be devastating if you are not properly covered in a church. Don't waste your time or energy fighting with other people – this battle is won on your knees.

Your armor

13 Therefore put on the full armor of God, so that when the day of evil comes, you may be able to stand your ground, and after you have done everything, to stand.

We live in that difficult time between Christ's victory on the cross and the full manifestation of His kingdom when He returns. Things may be calm for you now, but the sense of this verse is, "Get ready now, and learn how to use your armor and resist the enemy." There are very evil days ahead, and if you are not prepared, you will not be able to resist him, and you will fall in the battle.

God has given you everything you need to resist and overcome the enemy's attacks. Satan can be brutal, but you can make it, standing firm in Jesus. God has done His part: He has given you the armor and weapons you need. Now you have to do your part. You can have the best weapons around, but if you do not know how to use them, or if they are at home when you run into trouble in the street, they are no good. Put on your armor.

Once again, I want to stress that Paul is not advising us to go out and pick a fight with the devil. Satan will come, and he will attack you. God protects you from his attacks and gives you the strength to resist. Your part is to stand firm and resist him.

Are you standing strong? Or are you full of doubt and discouragement, tossed all over the place? In the following chapters, we will study each piece of your armor. Have you used it in the past? What has been your experience with it? Have you been deceived into wrestling with flesh and blood? Be careful! Hold on, and seek the Lord. You do not want to wound a loved one, or waste your time shadow boxing. Are you resisting a satanic attack right now? Or have you already given up? Are you tired of the struggle? God wants to renew your strength! Now is not the time to give up! Victory may be right around the corner! God is with you, and will help you!

21   YOUR ARMOR: TRUTH & RIGHTEOUSNESS

EPHESIANS 6:14

For forty years, I have been reading Ephesians 6. I have preached it many times. I know how important this armor is. But I still have this uneasy feeling that I do not fully understand it or fully utilize it, and I suspect I am not alone. I have seen cute pictures of a soldier dressed in each piece – but how many really are putting on the armor every day?

14 Stand firm then, with the belt of truth buckled around your waist, with the breastplate of righteousness in place.

Stand therefore [hold your ground], having tightened the belt of truth around your loins and having put on the breastplate of integrity and of moral rectitude and right standing with God. (AMP)

I don't know about you, but my loins are pretty important to me, as well as being very sensitive to attack. That, along with the fact that Paul puts this first, gives truth a very important place. The objective here is not preparing to fight; it is doing what is necessary to stand your ground and not be moved or knocked down as all these evil forces come against you. Satan is a deceiver and the father of lies. His attacks usually start with doubt, confusion, and disorientation; you do not know what to think or what to believe anymore. Jesus said they would get even worse in the last days. Many believers are not sure of what is true, and have their doubts about the Bible. Our culture declares that there is no absolute truth, no right and wrong, and that those who claim there is are arrogant and close-minded.

What is the truth?

Jesus answered, "I am the way and the truth and the life. No one comes to the Father except through me. (John 14:6)

The truth is a person, Jesus Christ. To be girded in the truth is to be dressed in Christ, abiding in Him, and walking in fellowship with Him. If you know the living God, you know the truth.

*So in Christ Jesus you are all children of God through faith, for all of you who were baptized into Christ have **clothed yourselves with Christ**.* (Galatians 3:26-27)

As you put on your armor and gird your loins, think about your baptism, and how that water covered you. You came up out of those waters dressed in Christ. Think about being clothed like that all day.

*And I will ask the Father, and he will give you another advocate to help you and be with you forever— **the Spirit of truth**.* (John 14:16-17)

You have an amazing resource in discerning the truth: The Spirit of truth who dwells within you. If you are walking in the Spirit, He will protect you from lies and deceit. Remember the second step we studied, in Ephesians 4 & 5, and the importance of the Spirit? If you have not learned how to live in His fullness, you will find it hard to know the truth.

*Sanctify them by the truth; **your word is truth**.* (John 17:17)

We also have the written truth, in the Bible. Unfortunately, many of the most dogmatic purveyors of that written truth seem to lack the personal relationship with the truth (in Jesus and the Spirit), giving truth a bad name. You need both. Study the Word to learn the truth. Evaluate everything you hear in light of that Word. Reject the lies that fill the world today.

*You will know how people ought to conduct themselves in God's household, which is **the church of the living God, the pillar and foundation of the truth**.* (I Timothy 3:15)

Once again, we see the importance of the church, the first stop on our journey to mature manhood. A true church preaches the Word of God and encourages people to walk in fellowship with the truth, Jesus Christ.

"If you hold to my teaching, you are really my disciples. Then you will know the truth, and the truth will set you free." (Jesus, John 8:31-32)

The world sees truth as being very rigid, and views those who believe there is truth and falsehood as intolerant fanatics. That is another of the devil's lies. Jesus said the truth will set you free. While many believe obedience and submission to God is bondage, Jesus said the only way to know the truth is to put His teachings into practice. As you do, God himself confirms that it is truth. To gird yourself with the truth you need to follow Jesus' teachings.

So the truth is not purely intellectual. Putting on truth is:

- Walking in union and communion with Jesus.
- Walking in the fullness of the Spirit of truth.

- Studying His Word and evaluating everything you experience in light of that Word.
- Being part of a church that teaches the Bible (the truth), and encourages you to walk in fellowship with Christ.
- Obeying God's Word.

In your circumstances right now, ask God, is there a lie I have accepted? Is my thinking about my life, my problems, and the Lord in line with the truth? If you are unsure if something is true, ask the Spirit of truth to show you. Renounce every lie, confessing where Satan has deceived you. Study the Bible to discover how God sees the situation. Declare your commitment to follow and live the truth.

The breastplate of righteousness

The breastplate protects your heart, not by your own righteousness, since your righteousness is as filthy rags, but by Christ's righteousness.

That I may be found in Christ, not having a righteousness of my own that comes from the law, but that which is through faith in Christ—the righteousness that comes from God on the basis of faith. (Philippians 3:9)

The devil will condemn you and call you a sinner – and in that, he is correct. You need Christ's righteousness. Many still try to be righteous through the law, working as hard as they can to be good Christians – and end up self-righteous. They are very religious. They do not smoke or drink, and they carefully follow a whole set of mostly man-made rules. But they are still under the law. Their righteousness does not come from faith. They tend to be Pharisees. To put on the breastplate we have to confess our sin and receive Christ's righteousness, by faith. If you insist on trying to obtain righteousness through good works, your armor will not work.

The Lord looked and was displeased
  that there was no justice.
He saw that there was no one,
  he was appalled that there was no one to intervene;
so his own arm achieved salvation for him,
  and his own righteousness sustained him.
He put on righteousness as his breastplate,
  and the helmet of salvation on his head;
he put on the garments of vengeance
  and wrapped himself in zeal as in a cloak. (Isaiah 59:12-17)

Isn't it interesting that the armor was prophesied in Isaiah – and Christ was the first to use this breastplate of righteousness? His righteousness will sustain you! Thank Him for this great gift of salvation!

But since we belong to the day, let us be sober, putting on faith and love as a breastplate, and the hope of salvation as a helmet. (I Thessalonians 5:8)

This verse sounds like a variation on the passage we are studying. The breastplate could be righteousness, love, or faith. As we just saw, we receive Christ's righteousness through faith. In doing so you receive His love, which provides even more protection from the devil's attacks.

Righteousness and integrity are your basic equipment. Every time you sin, a small chink appears in your armor. Any darkness in your life attracts demons and their powers of darkness.

To put on this breastplate of righteousness:

- Confess any sin in your life aloud. Be especially sensitive to subtle sins. Name them, agree with God that they are sin, and renounce them.

- Tell God that you want no part of that sin, whether it is a thought, feeling, or action. Tell Him you are sorry you allowed it in your life, because you know it violates His righteousness. There is worldly sorrow that produces death; avoid that. Only godly sorrow produces repentance.

- Thank Him that the sin was judged at Calvary and its power broken at the cross.

- Thank God for the blood of Jesus, which cleanses you from all sin.

This is the message we have heard from him and declare to you: God is light; in him there is no darkness at all. If we claim to have fellowship with him and yet walk in the darkness, we lie and do not live out the truth. But if we walk in the light, as he is in the light, we have fellowship with one another, and the blood of Jesus, his Son, purifies us from all sin.

If we claim to be without sin, we deceive ourselves and the truth is not in us. If we confess our sins, he is faithful and just and will forgive us our sins and purify us from all unrighteousness. If we claim we have not sinned, we make him out to be a liar and his word is not in us. (I John 1:5-10)

The way to God's righteousness starts with the truth, which is why you put that on first. Agree that you are a sinner, confess the sin, forsake it, and rejoice in Christ's forgiveness and righteousness.

22   Your armor: The Gospel of Peace

Ephesians 6:15

Your loins are girded with truth, and the breastplate of righteousness is protecting your heart. Now you are ready for your shoes. *Therefore, since we have been justified through faith, we have peace with God through our Lord Jesus Christ.* (Romans 5:1)

Being at peace with God and having inner peace is great protection from the devil's attacks, and he runs away even faster when we proclaim the Gospel. The Gospel, and the peace it brings, is the solid rock we stand on. All other ground is sinking sand.

[15] Stand firm then, with your feet fitted with the readiness that comes from the gospel of peace.

Stand therefore [hold your ground], having shod your feet in preparation [to face the enemy with the firm-footed stability, the promptness, and the readiness produced by the good news] of the Gospel of peace. (AMP)

This may be the most difficult piece of armor to define precisely. What we do know is:

- It has to do with shoes and our feet, which could imply movement, stability, or protection.   Since the exhortation in verse 14 was to *stand firm,* these shoes probably are not about movement. Perhaps Paul was thinking of the spiked sandals Roman soldiers wore, that dug into the ground to keep their footing in battle. The foundation of the Gospel provides you with firm footing.

- Something about it prepares you for any situation. There is no time to take your shoes off and sleep; be ready to live and proclaim the Gospel. Satan hates hearing the Gospel, and will run the other way when you preach it.

- The focus here is the Good News of salvation in Christ. Satan always tries to distract us from the pure Gospel. Fight to keep your footing there.

- The Gospel brings peace with God and with other people. Division and discord are usually the work of the enemy. If you are not at peace with your wife or other people, you will be much more vulnerable to his attacks.

How beautiful on the mountains are the feet of those who bring good news, who proclaim peace, who bring good tidings, who proclaim salvation, who say to Zion, "Your God reigns!" (Isaiah 52:7)

Paul may have been thinking of that verse when he wrote this. If you are busy sharing the good news, you will experience God's joy and favor, and Satan will have a harder time getting to you.

Our most common battles are with other people: your spouse, your kids, your parents, your boss – even brothers in the church. But the Gospel brings peace to homes and communities. Are you an instrument of peace in your school? Your home? At work?

Lack of forgiveness will rob you of peace. Ask God if there is someone you have not truly forgiven. If there is, tell God aloud that, in obedience, you are choosing to forgive him – even if he does not deserve it. Thank God that He has forgiven you, just as you have forgiven the other person.

Do you have peace? Jesus said *Peace I leave with you; my peace I give you. I do not give to you as the world gives. Do not let your hearts be troubled and do not be afraid.* (John 14:27) Jesus gives peace. It is a gift, deeper than the world's peace, and unrelated to circumstances. It is the Jewish *Shalom* – a state of total well-being. A troubled or cowardly soldier will not fight well. Christ's peace guards against anguish and cowardice. If you still feel troubled, try this advice from Philippians 4:6-7: *Do not be anxious about anything, but in every situation, by prayer and petition, with thanksgiving, present your requests to God. And the peace of God, which transcends all understanding, will guard your hearts and your minds in Christ Jesus.*

23   YOUR ARMOR: THE SHIELD OF FAITH
EPHESIANS 6:16

In addition to all this, take up the shield of faith, with which you can extinguish all the flaming arrows of the evil one.

Lift up over all the [covering] shield of saving faith, upon which you can quench all the flaming missiles of the wicked [one]. (AMP)

The first three pieces of armor have to do with *who you are*. They enable you to get a firm footing.   Once you are established, you are ready to take a more active role in this battle. The first words of the verse literally are *in all* or *over all*, indicating that this may be one of the most important pieces of your armor. Without this shield, you are still very vulnerable, and will experience constant ups and downs. Those flaming arrows will go right into your heart. Many Christians walk around wounded because of them, but that is not necessary. With this shield, you not only *stop* Satan's flaming missiles, you *quench*, or *extinguish*, them. This is one very useful piece of armor!

What are some of the flaming arrows that can wound you?

- Doubts.
- Fears.
- Reminders of your weaknesses and sin.

- Depression and discouragement.
- All kinds of temptations, often subtle.

Notice your responsibility: God wants to train you in warfare. He certainly could fight your battles – and there are times when He will. But He also wants you to grow up and learn how to fight your own battles. You do not want your son to stay a little kid forever, do you? It may be cute for a six year old to come running to daddy to help him fight. But it is tragic if he is still doing that when he is 25. You want him to learn how to deal with life.

How does the shield work?

- You must be vigilant. For the shield to work you have to be alert and see the arrow coming before it hits your heart. Once you have been wounded, it takes time to heal. Learn how and when the enemy attacks you with those flaming missiles.
- Many of his most lethal arrows come from those we love most. She may not know it or do it on purpose, but your wife's words penetrate deep into your heart. There may be times when you almost make yourself a target, giving up without a struggle, letting the arrow hit your heart and meditating on the hurt. Don't do it. For example, she might say to you, "You don't love me. I'm going to leave you for a real man." At that point, do not get into a fight or try to defend yourself. Simply lift up your shield of faith as soon as you see the arrow coming: "I vowed before God to love you for the rest of my life. I know I am not perfect, but God is changing me. He hates divorce and so do I. God has made us one

flesh, and no matter what happens, I'm going to keep on loving you."

The nature of faith

Faith is not some force that gives you what you want; faith is based on who God is and what He has said in his Word. Faith comes by hearing, and hearing by the Word of God. If you fill your mind with worldly thoughts, your shield will not work. Mediate on the Word and proclaim it in faith.

Now faith is confidence in what we hope for and assurance about what we do not see. (Hebrews 11:1)

Now faith is the assurance of things hoped for, the conviction of things not seen. (AMP)

Meditate on Hebrews 11 for examples of men and women of faith. Note the flaming arrows the enemy launched at them – and how they extinguished them with their faith.

In Mark 4 (verse 35), Jesus said to his disciples, *"Let's cross to the other side of the lake."* But half way across, arrows of fear and doubt came straight at them. They forgot about whom they were with and what He had said. They got scared and accepted the lie that God did not care about them: *"Teacher, don't you care that we're going to drown?"* After rebuking the waves, Jesus said to them *"Why are you so afraid? Do you still have no faith?"* They were not using the shield of faith to extinguish the arrows of their circumstances. They were walking by sight and not by faith. And with their hearts wounded, they were in no shape to rise up and rebuke the wind and waves.

Do you have faith?

Life is going to be tough if you do not have faith. Satan's flaming missiles will constantly wound you. Wake up! Examine yourself to see where you have been wounded. You do not have to get into big battles with the devil or rebuke him. Simply lift up the shield of faith and quench those fiery arrows – before they can get to your heart. Learn to discern what they look like, and how to use your shield to extinguish them. It is better than a video game! *Above all, take up the shield of faith.* God wants you to be a mature man, not a kid tossed about on the waves.

24 Your armor: The Helmet of Salvation & the Sword of the Spirit

Ephesians 6:17

Put on salvation as your helmet, and take the sword of the Spirit, which is the word of God. (NLT)

Your helmet

Are you saved? Are you sure? Remember our study on salvation in chapter 11, almost at the beginning of these steps to maturity? If you are not saved, your head is unprotected. But if you are saved, you are an adopted child of God. God has given you eternal life. This helmet protects your mind from doubts about your salvation.

The word translated *salvation* can also be translated *deliverance*. If the enemy still has strongholds in your life, it will be very difficult to walk in victory. You will wander around in darkness and confusion. Christ came to save you and deliver you from the devil's oppression. The helmet protects you from his lies and deceit. Do not be discouraged or give up. No matter what your situation, there is hope for deliverance.

First Thessalonians 5:8-9 also speaks of a helmet: *But since we belong to the day, let us be sober, putting on faith and love as a breastplate, and the hope of salvation as a helmet. For God did not appoint us to suffer wrath but to receive salvation through our Lord Jesus Christ.* The focus here is on the hope our salvation gives us, freeing us from the fear of judgment, and giving us security. Satan cannot steal your salvation. Almost like an umbrella, this helmet covers everything else.

Revelation 12: 10 gives us a broad vision of this salvation:

"Now have come the salvation and the power
  and the kingdom of our God,
  and the authority of his Messiah.
For the accuser of our brothers and sisters,
  who accuses them before our God day and night,
  has been hurled down."

With salvation come power, authority, and kingdom dominion. When you are saved, you enter God's kingdom and receive that power and authority from the King. At the same time, the accuser is cast out of your life. The helmet protects you from his accusations. Rise up in the power of Christ and take authority over every troubling thought.

Without this helmet, the obvious alternatives are suicide, or falling into sin. When you start contemplating either, you know you are under intense spiritual attack. Quickly grab this helmet and remind yourself of your salvation and deliverance in Christ. Better yet, keep it on at all times so those thoughts do not come! Then thank God that He sent Jesus as an atoning sacrifice for your sin, to forgive you and set you free from the kingdom of darkness.

Your sword

The word of God is alive and active. Sharper than any double-edged sword, it penetrates even to dividing soul and spirit, joints and marrow; it judges the thoughts and attitudes of the heart. (Hebrews 4:12)

The sword of the Spirit, the Word of God, is your only offensive weapon. Memorize the Bible. Study it. Meditate on it. Proclaim it and obey it. A Bible on the shelf does you no good. It must be in your heart and available in the heat of battle.

As you use your sword, remember:

- The devil also knows the Word. He used it to tempt Jesus. It is very possible to abuse the Word.
- To be a sword of the Spirit it must be correctly interpreted. It is important to learn how to understand it.
- For the sword to be effective, you must be full of the Spirit. Do not grieve Him or quench Him with sin. There is supernatural anointing on the Word when a believer correctly proclaims it in faith.
- The sword is almost at the end of the armor. If you do not have the other pieces in place, you will still suffer in battle. For example, if there is sin in your life and the breastplate of righteousness is not in place, or if you are not saved and protected by the helmet, the sword is not going to do you much good.
- I have seen plenty of people use the Bible as a sword – but not walk in love, truth, or righteousness. They hurt

many people, but they do not do much damage to the kingdom of darkness.

There is an alarming lack of biblical knowledge today. Many Christians do not have their sword, and I am not talking about carrying Bibles, because multitudes have it on their smart phones. But they do not know what it says or how to use it as a sword. God wants to teach you how to use your sword. This is a true adventure – far better than any video game.

There is just one more piece of armor, which will serve as glue bringing all the rest together.

25   YOUR ARMOR: PRAYER

EPHESIANS 6:18

With all prayer and petition pray at all times in the Spirit, and with this in view, be on the alert with all perseverance and petition for all the saints. (NASB)

Pray at all times (on every occasion, in every season) in the Spirit, with all [manner of] prayer and entreaty. To that end keep alert and watch with strong purpose and perseverance, interceding in behalf of all the saints (God's consecrated people). (AMP)

Right along with the Word comes prayer. For your prayer to be effective in this battle it should be:

- **Continuous.** We would love to rationalize that Paul *surely* did not mean at *all* times –even though that is clearly what he said. That constant connection with your Commander in Chief, with God, is essential if you are going to survive this battle. Satan is determined to destroy you. It is worth your while to take him seriously, and do what the Bible tells you to do. Most Christians seem to think that ten or fifteen minutes of prayer a day should do it, and then they wonder why they live in defeat, oppressed by the enemy.

- **Prayer and *petition*, or *entreaty*.** Apparently, there is a shade of difference between the two. Prayer may simply be fellowship with God, while entreaty, or supplication, suggests a more focused, urgent, calling out to God. It also carries the idea of humility and submission. Remember how important submission was in the third step to maturity? A submissive attitude toward God will also have a big impact on your prayer. It is fine to be bold in prayer, but it's not your place to boss God around. As you pray, remember that God is sovereign, and pray humbly and submissively.

- **In the Spirit.** Certainly, that means guided by the Spirit, but I believe it means much more. A careful study of 1 Corinthians 14 shows that when Paul talks about praying in the Spirit, he almost certainly means praying in a prayer language. I know some Christians feel uncomfortable about that, but maybe it is time to put those perceptions aside and be open to all God has for us to help in this battle. Personally, many times in the heat of battle I do not know how to pray, or even feel like praying. But at that moment, the Spirit helps me in my weakness, and I call out to God in tongues. I can pray silently in tongues all day long. Try it! Tongues is a tremendous blessing for your prayer life.

- **Alert.** Watch and pray. Remember what happened to the disciples the night of Jesus' arrest? (Matthew 26:40) They could not keep watch for even an hour! Wake up! Sometimes you need to open your eyes as you pray and take a good look at what is happening around you.

- **Persevering**. Jesus taught the importance of perseverance in various parables (Luke 11:5-13 & 18:1-8).

  o Some battles last months – even years. They test your faith and perseverance. If you have been praying for the salvation of your parents or children for years, keep on praying and trusting in the Lord.

  o I have heard teachings that you should just ask once and then give thanks to God that it is done. There may be some truth in that, but it goes against Jesus' stress on the importance of perseverance and continuing in prayer until you receive an answer.

- **Pray for all believers**. You are not alone in this battle. You need the church's support (remember the first step?). Right now, there may be someone in the battle about to fall if nobody intercedes for them. Sharing your requests helps and encourages others to pray for you, and enables them to obey this command.

  o This prayer is supposed to be for *all the saints* – not just your friends, family, or church members. Find out what is going on in other countries and pray for them as well.

The word *all* is used four times here: At *all* times, in *all* prayer, with *all* perseverance, for *all* the saints. Ten minutes a day will not do it. Praying before meals and calling out to God in emergencies will not bring you victory in this fierce battle.

Prayer simply must have a central place in your life. It is your connection with God's power.

26 THE PRAYER OF A MATURE MAN

EPHESIANS 6:19-20

We have come to the end of Ephesians and these four steps to mature manhood. Do not get discouraged if you do not feel like you have "arrived" yet! This is a long process – life-long, to be exact! It may take years to get established in a church and get through the first step, but it's well worth it! Be patient! You may end up going back through the same steps over and over again. That is okay! Unfortunately, it is not as if you finish one step and you have that down for the rest of your life. Examine yourself frequently to see how you are doing on each step.

Paul has wrapped up his teaching, but in these two verses, we see the heart of a mature man. Not that he has achieved "perfection" or full maturity; Paul always was aware that he was on a pilgrimage to heaven and would never "arrive" in this life.

19 Pray also for me, that whenever I speak, words may be given me so that I will fearlessly make known the mystery of the gospel.

And pray for me, too. Ask God to give me the right words so I can boldly explain God's mysterious plan that the Good News is for Jews and Gentiles alike. (NLT)

The importance of praying for others

Paul was acutely aware of the importance of prayer. He would probably say he was alive and saved because others had prayed for him. He never assumed his ministry was a result of his own talent. He relied on the prayers of the church to receive a word given by the Lord, and preach it with anointing.

You are not alone in this struggle; you are part of a great army. Part of being in that army is supporting each other in prayer. Are you praying for your pastor and other Christian workers? If you are in ministry, humble yourself and ask for prayer. Let them know that without God's help you would be nothing.

Do not make a pastor or preacher an idol. They are men just like you and me, with their needs and weaknesses. They rely on God's grace to make an impact on this world.

The message

There is important teaching in Paul's request:

- First, you have to open your mouth. True, there are times when you need to wait for a word from the Lord, but there are also times when you need to open your mouth and trust God to fill it.

- There are also some who should close their mouths; they talk too much, and in the flesh. The mature man knows when to speak, and when to remain silent.

- When you speak, say what *God* has given you. Regrettably, many preachers say what the internet has given them, or what comes out of their own thinking.

- It may not be popular, but that is fine. It is God's Word, not yours. Knowing that God has given you the message should fill you with boldness to proclaim it, although even the great apostle Paul had to ask prayer for boldness! That anointing is God's gift.

- The focus of your message should be the Bible, the Gospel. Make its meaning clear. For many people the Bible remains a mystery. You cannot grasp it intellectually, but God wants to reveal it to those who have ears to hear.

- The message is for everyone. Paul fought his whole life for Gentiles to be included in the church. The Kingdom of God is for anyone who accepts the Gospel.

[20] *I am an ambassador in chains [for the Gospel]. Pray that I may declare it fearlessly, as I should.*

I am in chains now, still preaching this message as God's ambassador. So pray that I will keep on speaking boldly for him, as I should. (NLT)

Do you think you have it rough? Paul was in prison, but his prayer was to speak boldly for the Lord. Twice he asked for that boldness, even though that very boldness landed him in jail! It would be tempting just to stay quiet, but the mature man enters into battle in the Name of his Lord, ready to lay down his life for the Gospel. Do you boldly talk about Jesus at home, on the job, or at school, no matter what your situation is?

Paul had a great self-image. He was an ambassador for Christ! And you are too! (2 Corinthians 5:20) Is that how you see yourself? Do you act like an ambassador of the King of kings? As we end this study of growing toward maturity, Paul was dedicated to his calling as a representative of Jesus Christ in this world. What is your calling? Are you busy serving God, despite your circumstances?

27 THE END OF THE STORY: THE MOST IMPORTANT IS LOVE
EPHESIANS 6:21-24

Paul's last words in this letter, his greetings, show us what really lasts, what is truly important:

- People.
- Relationships.
- Love - for God and for others.
- Doing everything possible to maintain those relationships.

[21] Tychicus, the dear brother and faithful servant in the Lord, will tell you everything, so that you also may know how I am and what I am doing. [22] I am sending him to you for this very purpose, that you may know how we are, and that he may encourage you.

[21] To bring you up to date, Tychicus will give you a full report about what I am doing and how I am getting along. He is a beloved brother and faithful helper in the Lord's work. [22] I have sent him to you for this very purpose—to let you know how we are doing and to encourage you. (NLT)

Paul wants them to know how he is doing. This is long before Facebook or the telephone. They depended on personal visits or letters that could take months to arrive. What a blessing to receive visitors, bringing news of beloved brothers! Do you stay in touch with brothers throughout the world? The internet has made it very easy! Are you interested in what is happening with them? Or are you so caught up in your own life that you really do not care?

It can be tempting to whitewash the news to include only the blessings and victories, but Tychicus will tell them *everything*. It is encouraging and comforting to get news about other brothers, hearing the testimonies of God's greatness and grace in their lives. Could you bless others with news about what God has done in you or your church?

Have you heard of Tychicus? His name means chance, or fortuitous, or fortunate. Some traditions include him in a list of seventy apostles in the early church. He appears several times in the New Testament:

- *[Paul] was accompanied by Sopater son of Pyrrhus from Berea, Aristarchus and Secundus from Thessalonica, Gaius from Derbe, Timothy also, and Tychicus and Trophimus from the province of Asia.* (Acts 20:4) He was with Paul on his journey through Greece and Macedonia, and part of the way back to Jerusalem. He probably went home (likely in Ephesus) as they passed through Asia.

- *Tychicus will tell you all the news about me. He is a dear brother, a faithful minister and fellow servant in the Lord.* (Colossians 4:7) Possibly on the same trip to Ephesus, Tychicus visited Colossae. Just as Paul was an ambassador of Christ, Tychicus was Paul's ambassador (and an ambassador of Christ).

- *Only Luke is with me. Get Mark and bring him with you, because he is helpful to me in my ministry. I sent Tychicus to Ephesus.* (2 Timothy 4:11-12) In his letter to Timothy, we learn that Paul has already sent Tychicus to Ephesus. He had been with Paul in Rome. The brother was well traveled!

- *As soon as I send Artemas or Tychicus to you, do your best to come to me at Nicopolis, because I have decided to winter there.* (Titus 3:12) Once again, we see how much Paul trusted Tychicus to carry out his wishes.

What a blessing to have someone like Tychicus! Could you be a Tychicus to a Paul? Do you have a trustworthy helper like Tychicus? Thank God for him, and do not take him for granted!

23 Peace to the brothers and sisters, and love with faith from God the Father and the Lord Jesus Christ. 24 Grace to all who love our Lord Jesus Christ with an undying love.

23 Peace be with you, dear brothers and sisters, and may God the Father and the Lord Jesus Christ give you love with faithfulness. 24 May God's grace be eternally upon all who love our Lord Jesus Christ. (NLT)

Here Paul puts a condition on experiencing God's grace: You must love Jesus with an undying love. Do you have that kind of love for Christ?

Together, as part of the divine trinity, the Father and Son grant us peace, love, and faith. Are you lacking one or more of those? God knows they do not come naturally, but He is ready to give us what we lack.

These verses are full of God's love:

- Love among brothers.
- A servant's love for the great apostle Paul.
- Paul's love for Timothy and the church in Ephesus.
- Our love for God.
- And God's love poured out in our hearts.

Do you know that love? As we will see in Revelation, that love is very important!

Returning to the History of the Church in Ephesus:

They Risk Losing Everything!

28   THE EPHESIANS LEFT THEIR FIRST LOVE

REVELATION 2:1–7

Unfortunately, we finish this study of four steps to mature manhood with a warning: The Ephesians forgot what was most important. Like many of us, they worked hard. They did everything right. They won many battles. But they lost the war.

In his letter to the Corinthians, Paul said you can do great miracles and even lay down your life, but if you do not have love, it means nothing. In the midst of all their services and activities, the Ephesians had left their first love.

"To the angel of the church in Ephesus write:

These are the words of him who holds the seven stars in his right hand and walks among the seven golden lampstands. I know your deeds, your hard work and your perseverance. I know that you cannot tolerate wicked people, that you have tested those who claim to be apostles but are not, and have found them false. You have persevered and have endured hardships for my name, and have not grown weary.

Yet I hold this against you: You have forsaken the love you had at first. Consider how far you have fallen! Repent and do the things you did at first. If you do not repent, I will come to you and remove your lampstand from its place. But you have this in your favor: You hate the practices of the Nicolaitans, which I also hate.

Whoever has ears, let them hear what the Spirit says to the churches. To the one who is victorious, I will give the right to eat from the tree of life, which is in the paradise of God.

(Revelation 2:1-7)

Yes, by the grace of God, they had remained steadfast in their faith. At the end of the first century, it was a large, active, church, known for its many good deeds. They had worked tirelessly for the sake of Jesus' name. There was fruit of the Spirit, like patience. They persevered in the face of great trials. They would not tolerate evil. They tested leaders of the church. Like today, some claimed to be apostles, but were not. They were diligent in discerning the truth and exposing falsehood.

They hated the practices of the Nicolaitans, who took sin lightly, especially sexual sin. Notice it says they hated *what they did* – not the people. We must hate what God hates. It really is okay to hate sin, but be sure to love the person.

Yes, in many ways this was an exemplary church. It would probably compare with the best of the mega churches today. But there was one glaring problem: They had left their first love. They had held an exalted position and been richly blessed. But they had fallen – without even realizing it. They have to repent, because losing your love for God is a sin. Nothing else really matters. The first commandment is to love God. They were so busy doing ministry and battling the devil that they lost that place of intimacy with Jesus. They have to return to their first works.

If they do not, they could lose their lampstand. That means it would no longer be a true church in God's eyes. There are many churches like Ephesus, with lots of programs and great music and beautiful buildings – but no life. God's Spirit is not there. They have lost their lampstand because they have left their first love, or allowed sin in their midst. The church is dead. They do not lose their salvation, but they lose the presence and power of Jesus in their midst.

Whether you realize it or not, the battle is on for your life and your church. Satan wants to destroy you, your family, and your church. We have studied four steps to mature manhood. Participating in a healthy church, walking in holiness, and laying down your life for your family are very important. More than ever, you need the spiritual armor, the Sword of the Spirit, and the shield of faith. Too many have been wounded by the enemy's flaming darts. But in the midst of all this, the first command is still to love God with all your heart and maintain that intimate relationship with God. How is your love? Are you in danger of losing your lampstand?

THE NEXT STEP

It is very evident from this study that God designed us to live in community. To reach mature manhood, you need your brothers. But it is also obvious that this book is not for every man; unfortunately, few men want to do the hard work of reaching maturity. They prefer to stick with their routine, their sports, and their comfortable lives. Some, however, long for something more. Some long for the solid food of the Word. It is those men I believe God wants to join together to follow these steps.

Four Step Men

I know it is easier to wait for someone else to take the initiative, but you may be the vessel God wants to use to transform your family, church, or community. How do you start?

1. Ask God to show you and bring you hungry men who are ready to receive this teaching.
2. Loan them this book, or buy another one and give it to them. (If you bought a print copy through Amazon, you can get a free digital copy.) You may already have a men's group in your church, or a group of elders, or your own sons.
3. Make a covenant (see below) to meet:
    a. Share your successes and failures.
    b. Pray for each other.
    c. Talk about how to put these steps into practice.
    d. Confidentiality and honesty are very important in these meetings.
4. Study this book together, or other books I have written, or my blogs (ASpiritualFather.com), or the Bible.

What about women?

I am not sexist, but I believe it is important for men to take the initiative to put these steps into practice. Your wife may be skeptical when she sees this book: "You? A mature man?" In some cases, it may be good to share what you are learning with her, but not always. Of course, the Bible applies to women as well, and God wants them to reach maturity. They should follow the same four steps, although they will look somewhat different:

- Their experience in the church will be different.
- Their struggles will be different; sex and anger are typically not as big problems for women.
- Their role in the family will be different.
- She is also in a spiritual battle, but the devil's strategy with women is different.

It could be worthwhile to talk about what these four steps would look like for her.

"But I'm not a pastor; I've never led a group before..."

No problem! This is God's Word, and God will surely do His part in helping you put it in practice. More than anyone else, He wants you to reach maturity! Write me and share your experiences with the four steps and your group (Loren@ASpiritualFather.com).

Covenant

Everyone in the group should sign this covenant and remove it from the book to keep in their Bibles (if they still have a print Bible!).

As brothers in Jesus Christ, we make a covenant to walk together and pursue these four steps to maturity, with God's help. I commit to praying and supporting my brothers, and being honest with them.

Signature   Date

_____

Other men in the group can also sign here, as an expression of unity:

www.ingramcontent.com/pod-product-compliance
Lightning Source LLC
Chambersburg PA
CBHW060234050426
42448CB00009B/1439